GURUS ON PEOPLE MANAGEMENT

SULTAN KERMALLY

Printed in 2004 and reprinted in 2008 by
Thorogood Publishing Ltd
10-12 Rivington Street
London EC2A 3DU

17 MAY 2013

12|13

Telephone: 020 7749 4748
Fax: 020 7729 6110
Email: info@thorogoodpublishing.co.uk
Web: www.thorogoodpublishing.co.uk

© Sultan Kermally 2004

A CIP catalogue record for this book is
available from the British Library.

PB: ISBN 1 85418 320 6

Cover and book designed by Driftdesign

Printed in the UK by Ashford Colour Press

About the Author

Sultan Kermally holds degrees in Economics, Sociology and Law and Diplomas in Finance & Accounting, Marketing and Education. He is a Learning facilitator and management writer. He designs and delivers training courses in Business Strategy, Managing People, Managing Performance, Managing Knowledge and Personal Development. He has conducted training in the UK, the Netherlands, Belgium, France, Austria, the Middle East, Hong Kong and Tajikistan.

For several years he has held senior academic positions in Scotland and thereafter, senior management positions with Management Centre Europe in Brussels, The London Business School and The Economist Group.

He has been involved in management education and development for a number of years, including distance learning management education courses. He is tutoring MBA modules on Strategy, Managing Knowledge Managing People, Strategic Marketing and International Business for the Open University Business School and Durham University Business School.

He is the author of ten management books including his latest book on *Effective Knowledge Management: A Best Practice Blueprint* published by Wiley under the CBI fast-track series and *Gurus on Marketing* and *Managing and Developing Talent* published by Thorogood.

He can be contacted by e-mail: Skermally@aol.com
www.sultankermally.me.uk

Acknowledgements

My sincere thanks go to Neil Thomas and Angela Spall for giving me an opportunity to contribute to their *Gurus on...* series.

I thank the following individuals, organisations and websites for the help received:

- David W. Creelman, Editor HR.Com.

- Belinda Pianezza, HR.Com Editor.

- Becky Whiley, Head of Marketing, Investors in People, UK.

- Suzanne Evans, PR Consultant to the Ken Blanchard Companies, UK. (Becky and Suzanne have been very helpful in providing appropriate information.)

- Ken Blanchard Companies, UK.

- Investors in People.

- Management Centre Europe, Brussels.

- Butterworth-Heinemann.

- The Macmillan Company.

- McGraw-Hill Publishing.

- www.actiondesign.com.

- www.leaderstoleader.com.

My love and thanks go to my wife Laura, my children Zara, Pete, Susan, Jenny, and my grandchildren Matthew, Anna and Eve.

My gratitude and special thanks go to my daughter Zara who, at the time of writing, is nearly four years old. She has been particularly helpful in 'demonstrating' the importance of needs and self-actualisation when I came to survey various motivational theories.

Contents

ONE
The challenges of managing people

"To see what you can be,
start with who you are."

ANON

Globalisation, empowerment, cross-functional teams, downsizing, restructuring, learning organisations, knowledge workers. If these buzzwords don't sound familiar, they should, they are changing your life and the way you manage people.

Managers have to manage people. I would say managing people constitutes at least 80% of the managerial function. It is the most difficult and yet most rewarding function. Most managers do not want to own up to the fact that they are inadequate as far as managing people are concerned. Even some organisations do not want to accept that all managers need continuous training and support in relation to their function of managing people.

When I was a Senior Director at Management Centre Europe, Brussels I devised and introduced a programme in 1987 called 'Managing People'. My senior colleagues and even my 'boss' was against the idea of such a programme because they felt organisations would not enrol their managers for such a course. The course got an approval and it ran once a year. By the time I left MCE in 1989 it was scheduled to run several times a year. I am given to understand that it is now one of the most popular programmes at MCE.

It became popular because, in my opinion, organisations and managers began to realise the importance of the skill of managing people, and that this skill needs to be sharpened on a continuous basis. Increasingly we live in a world where the rate of change is accelerating; goals are becoming more varied and complex and where knowledge as a key strategic asset is contributing to business success.

People are our greatest asset. Is this hype or reality? For those organisations who genuinely believe in their people, managing people becomes the foremost managerial skill.

Managing people is not a matter of manipulation. It is about working with your staff and colleagues on a partnership basis to achieve the strategic goals of the organisation.

The success of an organisation depends on managing three sets of expectations. They are:

- organisational expectations;
- employee expectations; and
- customer expectations.

What does managing employee expectations involve? It involves **understanding** and the subsequent application of the following:

- Understanding of human needs and behaviour.
- What makes people tick?
- How to form collaborative relationships.
- How to recruit and select staff.
- Understanding the nature of psychological contract.
- How to retain staff.
- How to formulate performance goals involving your staff.
- How to monitor and measure staff performance.
- How to lead and motivate staff.
- How to communicate effectively with your staff.

- How to develop talent in your organisation.

- How to make your staff work effectively in teams.

- How to empathise with your staff.

- How to act as a mentor or a coach.

- The nature of change.

- The significance of work-family balance.

- How to gain commitment from your staff.

- How to create a thriving work environment.

- Above all, understanding self.

This is a very daunting task but it is imperative to acquire competences in all these aspects to manage effectively. In practice various dimensions of managing people and the importance of people in bringing about organisational success, come together in different forms.

Listen for possibilities

"If you should try to understand me
Through the eyes of your experiences,
Your only understanding will be
Misunderstanding.
For we have walked different paths
And have known different fears.
And that which brings you laughter just
Might bring me tears.

So if you can learn to accept me
And the strange things I say and do,
Maybe through your acceptance
You will gain understanding."

Anon.

People management issues in practice

Chapter 18 of this book introduces some case studies that reflect some of the issues of managing people. These are national and international case studies.

(Disclaimer: I have no relationship whatsoever with the organisations which have supplied case studies. I use them to highlight and reinforce different dimensions of managing people involved in practice.)

Continuous improvement

It is also important to constantly review motivational and leadership factors involved in enhancing organisational effectiveness, irrespective of how successful you are at present. If a successful organisation like Dell finds it necessary to do so, so should other organisations.

So what has Dell done? The following is an article which appeared in Management Centre Europe E-Newsletter written by the author.

Managing by principles – Dell's way

By Sultan Kermally, freelance writer and management author.

In Business Week 0f November 3, 2003, there is a cover story on Dell entitled 'What You Don't Know About Dell'. In this article the writers highlight the following six management principles Dell have adopted and presented them as 'Management secrets of the best-run company in technology'. These principles are:

- Be direct.
- Leave the ego at the door.
- No excuses.
- No easy targets.
- No victory laps.
- Worry about saving money, not saving face.

How do these principles translate into developing and managing talent in your organisation and enable you to formulate a talent development strategy?

BE DIRECT

According to the writers, workers are supposed to challenge their bosses and question everything. What lessons can organisations learn from this principle?

In practice this has implications in terms of recruitment and development.

organisations at the recruitment stage should look for potential employees who have a challenging attitude. Choosing an expert in the field is fine but testing for interpersonal communication is also important. However, one should aim at selecting individuals with a challenging mindset. This is all about individual attitude and encouraging such an attitude within the context of corporate culture that facilitates promoting such an attitude.

LEAVE THE EGO AT THE DOOR

According to the Business Week article Dell "favours 'two-in-a-box' management in which two executives share responsibility for product, a region, or a company function."

This is about working in a team and as a team member. According to Peter Senge, the 'guru' of Learning organisation, collective knowledge is created by working in teams. However, being a team member is not enough. What matters is individual attitude towards the concept of team work? One has to be trained to understand the importance of team dynamics and participate in productive dialogues and discussion. An 'I am important' or 'I am an expert' attitude leads toone's ego preventing team learning and knowledge creation.

NO EXCUSES

This is about taking responsibility and being accountable for one's actions. Employees should have the courage to admit their weaknesses and take action to minimise or eliminate them. There should be no 'them syndrome'; it should be about asking the question 'What can I do to resolve the problem at hand?'. Again this requires a particular mindset and empowering culture. This is the true nature of empowerment.

NO EASY TARGETS

Employees must contribute to profit and growth. In practice this means incorporating stretch objectives in appraisal plans. S.M.A.R.T objectives in this case should be translated as Specific and stretch; Measurable and meaningful; Attainable and aligned; Realistic and time and Target related.

NO VICTORY LAPS

"The founder's mantra: 'Celebrate for a nanosecond, then move on'", say the writers.

There are numerous stories of many organisations having won total quality awards or 'Best company to work for' awards who drift into complacency.

Achievements should be followed by further achievements and this in practice necessitates implementation of the continuous improvement principle.

WORRY ABOUT SAVING MONEY, NOT SAVING FACE

Employees should be trained to 'pull the plug on disappointing new ventures'. Again, this requires a business mindset and tolerant culture. Face saving in modern organisations stifles innovation and stops what Peter Drucker called 'creative destruction'?

Dell's management principles are a reflection of five disciplines of the learning organisation presented by Peter Senge in his book 'The Fifth Discipline (1990). These five disciplines are:

1   Personal mastery (individual growth and learning).

2   Mental models (attitude and behaviour).

3   Shared vision (Direct and honest Communication).

4   Team learning (creating synergy within teams).

5   System thinking (seeing the big picture – organisational core competence).

Senge's five disciplines and Dell's six management principles direct organisations towards formulating talent development strategies focussing on three core components – **personal development, corporate culture and effective leadership.**

(Sultan Kermally is a freelance writer and management author. His book 'Managing and Developing Talent' will be published by Thorogood in 2004.) Source: Management Centre Europe.

The subsequent chapters relate to various 'gurus' on managing people. **The bottom line of managing people is motivation and leadership**. I have selected 14 gurus on four aspects of managing people, namely:

- motivation;

- leadership;

- culture; and

- knowledge.

In addition, I have included Charles Handy and Peter Drucker who have various contributions to make on different aspects of managing people. I had to be selective and since the field of managing people is so vast I have left out many academic and corporate gurus like Alderfer, Locke, Lawler, Schein, Pascale, Ulrich, Quinn, Trompenaars, Covey, John Harvey Jones, Jack Welch, Bill Gates, Andrew Grove, Arie de Geus and so on. Some may even include Dilbert in this list!

However, **the gurus selected represent all the key issues and dimensions of managing people effectively.**

TWO
Fredrick Winslow Taylor
(1856-1915)

"The search for better, for more competent men, from the presidents of our great companies down to our household servants, was never more vigorous than it is now. And more than ever before is the demand for competent men in excess of the supply.

What we are all looking for, however, is the ready-made, competent man; the man whom someone else has trained. It is only when we fully realise that our duty, as well as our opportunity, lies in systematically cooperating to train and to make this competent man, instead of in hunting for a man whom someone else has trained, that we shall be on the road to national efficiency."

FREDERIC TAYLOR: PRINCIPLES OF SCIENTIFIC MANAGEMENT, 1911

Guru's profile

Taylor is not a guru of managing people as such, but his contribution as a father of scientific management cannot be left out as it formed the foundation of management and subsequently of people management.

Frederick Taylor was born in 1856. His father was a lawyer and both his parents were Quakers and believed in plain living.

He was an industrial engineer and was trained in the basics of physical sciences. He got his engineering degree from Stevens Institute of Technology in New Jersey while still working full-time.

He worked in a metal products factory as a machinist, subsequently becoming a foreman. After six years he became research director and finally achieved the position of chief engineer.

Guru's contribution

Taylor's book, *The Principles of Scientific Management* published in 1911, advocated the development of the science of management with clearly stated rules and laws, scientific selection and training of workers, and the division of tasks and responsibilities between workers and management. Taylor recommended that there should be a detailed analysis of each job, using the techniques of method study and time study in order to find the method of working that would bring about the largest average rate of production, the so called *'one best way'*.

He also advocated issuing written instructions, training and incentive payments in order to ensure that jobs were performed in the approved manner.

In his testimony to the House of Representatives Committee, 1912, he articulated four principles of scientific management. These are:

1   The development of science for each element of a man's work to replace old methods. He advocated gathering of knowledge (mainly tacit knowledge of workmen) in order to enable the management side to manage effectively.

2   Secondly, he advocated scientific selection and training of workmen. He wrote "It becomes the duty of those on the management's side to deliberately study the character, the nature and the performance of each workmen with a view to finding out his limitations on the one hand, but even more important, his possibilities for development on the other hand; and then, as deliberately and as systematically to train, help and teach his workman, giving him, wherever it is possible, those opportunities for advancement which will finally enable him to do the highest and most interesting and most profitable class of work for which his natural abilities fit him, and which are open to him in the particular company in which he is employed."

3   Thirdly, he advocated the 'bringing together' of the science and scientifically selected workmen. He advocated cooperation between workers and management.

4   Finally, he advocated the fair and equal division of work between management and workers.

He reinforced his scientific principles by giving examples of pig-handling and shovelling. These examples came from the following experiments which he conducted:

He conducted his first experiment at Midvale Steel Company. *"He observed that each worker in a yard crew used his own shovel even though they sometimes shovelled ashes, sometimes iron ore and other times coal. This meant that the weight lifted per shovel load varied, depending on the particular material being moved. By experimenting, Taylor found that the most material was moved in a given period when* the payload of the shovel was about 21.5 pounds. He had the company buy an assortment of shovels so that the most appropriate size and shape of shovel could be used for the material being moved. In each case he made sure that the larger shovels used for ashes carried about 21.5 pounds and that the smaller ones used for iron are did the same. The immediate outcome of this simple change was increased output per worker.

The second experiment involved the workers who handled pig iron ingots in the same steel mill. After observing the worker he became convinced that output could be increased by improving handling methods. He believed the handlers were making the wrong movements, working too hard and too long, and resting too frequently. Taylor offered one of the workers a bonus if he would cooperate by following his directions on handling the pig iron and taking rest breaks. After following Taylor's directions the worker was able to increase his average daily movement of pig iron from 12.5 tons to 47 tons, an increase of nearly 300 per cent. At the same time, the pig iron carrier who participated in the experiment earned about 60 per cent more pay. The result was a lower labor cost per ton carried, even though the carrier earned more money per day." [1]

He believed that the secret of productivity was to find the right task for the person and then to give him financial incentive to increase productivity.

Taylor's influence in the area of management was enormous.

"Taylor's ideas were translated into practice remarkably quickly – particularly by Henry Ford, a self-made mechanic just like Taylor, at his new factory at Highland Park, in a suburb of Detroit. At the same time, Taylorism helped to shape the curriculum at a new sort of educational institution, the business school. The first business school, Wharton, was set up at the University of Pennsylvania in 1881. The University of Chicago and the University of California both established under-

---

1   Carvell, Fred J (1970). 'Human Relations in Business'. The Macmillan Company. Pp48

graduate schools of commerce in 1899. New York's University's Stern School of Business, Dartmouth's Amos Tuck School of Business Administration and Harvard Graduate School of Business Administration followed in the next decade. The Management Review was founded in 1918, the American Management Association in 1925. By end of the Great War, Arthur D. Little, originally an engineering firm, included management advice among its services. James McKinsey set up his consultancy firm in 1925."[2]

Drucker's views on scientific management

" ...Altogether it may well be the most powerful as well as the most lasting contribution America has made to Western thought since the Federalist Papers. As long as the industrial society endures, we shall never lose again the insight that human work can be studied systematically, can be analysed, can be improved by work on its elementary parts...Scientific management was thus one of the great liberating, pioneering insights. Without it a real study of human beings at work would be impossible. Without it we could never, in managing worker and work, go beyond good intentions, exhortations or the 'speed up'."[3]

Drucker also criticised Scientific Management as being very philosophical and engineering biased. It is engineering biased in the sense that it is believed that because we must analyse work into small motions it must also be organised in a series of small motions each performed by an individual worker. This is not logical. It considers workers to act as machines.

Scientific management also assumes that planning is distinct from doing. This is fine and it is one of Taylor's valuable insights. However, it does not mean that the planner and the door should be different people.

---

2   Micklethwait and Wooldridge (1996). 'The Witch Doctors'. Heinemann, London. Pp 74.

3   Drucker (1989). 'The Practice of Management'. Heinemann Professional Publishing. Pp274.

Taylor and managing people

Even though Taylor is not directly associated with ' Managing People' – his focus was on managing work and workers – he did draw attention to the importance of selection, training, compensation and motivation, the areas directly relevant to managing people in today's environment.

Lessons learnt from Frederick Winslow Taylor

- Employee problems are usually associated with poor organisation and management.

- Employee selection, training and compensation should be governed by scientific principles.

- Personalities and skills of employees play an important part in enhancing productivity.

- Group-made norms influence the behaviour of the employees.

- The development of each workman to his greatest physical capability.

- Management should work cooperatively in a supportive role.

Taylor's influence in the area of management was enormous.

THREE
Elton Mayo (1880-1949)

"Man's desire to be continuously associated in work with his fellows is a strong, if not the strongest, human characteristic. Any disregard of it by management or any ill-advised attempt to defeat this human impulse leads instantly to some form of defeat for management itself."

ELTON MAYO

Guru's profile

Elton Mayo, an Australian, was a professor of Industrial Research at the Harvard Graduate school of Business Administration.

He became famous for the Hawthorne studies which he conducted with his associates during the period of 1924 to 1932 at the Western Electric Hawthorne Works in Chicago.

He wrote his first book in 1933 called 'The Human Problems of an Industrial Civilisation'. In 1945 he published another book called The Social Problems of an Industrial Civilisation.

Guru's contribution

Mayo became famous for his experiments which were known as the **Hawthorne Experiments**. The main researchers were Fritz Roethlisberger and W. J. Dickson. These experiments were conducted at the Western Electric Hawthorne Works during the period 1924 to 1932.

His first experiment (1924-1927) looked at the effects of lighting on the productivity of workers in different departments of the company. He set out two rooms, one experimental and the other the control room. Changes were made in the intensity of lighting in the experimental room. The researchers first increased the light to an extreme brightness and then decreased the light until it was very dim. Regardless of the variations in the intensity of lighting, production increased. Production even increased in the control room when the lighting was constant.

The second experiment (1927-1929) was focused on the effects of rest periods on output. Five individuals were involved in this experiment. The experiment lasted three years and during this period the researchers found that there was an improved productivity every time changes were made.

Researchers concluded that the changes in productivity were not necessarily related to changes in physical working conditions.

The third experiment (1928-1930) involved the mass-interviewing of employees involved in various experiments. The researchers wanted to find out factors other than physical conditions which contributed to increased productivity. This experiment led researchers to conclude that morale was high during the experiment. The workers felt special because special attention was being paid to them. To be asked to participate in various experiments made them feel that someone was interested in them.

During the experiment period workers also formed good interpersonal relationships and they enjoyed working in groups. The researchers also found out that group dynamics and group norms contributed to increased productivity.

At interviewing stage *"it was speedily discovered that the question-and-answer type of interview was useless in the situation. Workers wished to talk, and to talk freely under the seal of professional confidence (which was never abused) to someone who seemed representative of the company or who seemed, by his very attitude, to carry authority. The experience itself was unusual; there are few people in this world who have had experience of finding someone intelligent, attentive and eager to listen, how to avoid interruption or the giving of advice, how generally to avoid anything that might put an end to free expression in an individual instance. Some approximate rules to guide the interviewer in his work were therefore set down. These were, more or less, as follows:*

1   *Give your whole attention to the person interviewed, and make it evident that you are doing so.*

2   *Listen – don't talk.*

3   *Never argue; never give advice.*

4   *Listen to:*

   • *What he wants to say.*

   • *What he does not want to say.*

   • *What he cannot say without help.*

5   *As you listen, plot out tentatively and for subsequent correction the pattern (personal) that is being set before you. To test this, from time to time summarise what has been said and present for comment (e.g. 'Is this what you are telling me?'). Always do this with the greatest caution, that is, clarify but do not add or distort.*

6   *Remember that everything said must be considered a personal*
     confidence and not divulged to anyone. (This does not prevent
     discussion of a situation between professional colleagues. Nor
     does it prevent some form of public report when due precau-
     tion been taken.)" [4]

These conclusions and observations led to the fourth experiment in 1932 – The Bank Wiring Observations Room experiment. This experiment involved 14 men employees divided into three sub-groups. These 14 men were removed from the main wiring area and were put in a special room. The working conditions in this room were the same as the working conditions in a main wiring room.

The researchers found that groups started developing their rules and behaviour and had norms for production level. The supervisors concerned were powerless to prevent this behaviour developing. Men who did not adhere to these norms and exceeded them were branded 'slaves' or 'speed kings'. Those who fell below the norms were called 'chiselers'. The group's production norms were more important than wage incentives.

The fifth and final experiment (1936) was conducted after The Bank Wiring Observation Room study. This experiment focused on improving company communication and provided an intensive counselling programme to workers to address employee relations.

Even though The Hawthorne Investigations made Elton Mayo famous, the official account of the experiments was written by one of his Harvard colleagues and one researcher.

---

4   Pugh, D. S. (Ed.) (1971). 'organisation Theory'. Penguin Education.

What conclusions can one draw from the Hawthorne Researches relating to managing people?

- organisations have a 'human' element.

- There is a strong relationship between worker morale and the quality of supervision.

- There are factors other than the work environment which affect worker motivation.

- Workers develop 'informal groups' within the organisation.

- These 'informal groups' play significant roles in influencing group members' behaviour.

- 'Informal groups' are more powerful than formal groups.

- Attitudes and feelings of workers influence productivity.

- People's behaviour may differ, depending on whether they are acting as a group or as individuals.

- We now talk about 'the Hawthorne Effect' to reflect the changing behaviour of workers when someone takes an interest in them.

- Mayo's experiments prompted many other subsequent studies on workers' morale, productivity and group dynamics.

- These experiments also have a bearing on subsequent studies on the types of leadership.

- It prompted the beginning of the Human Relations School of Management.

There have been many criticisms of the way the Hawthorne Experiments have been interpreted. Some say researchers adopted unreliable methods for validating the evidence presented. Most of the criticisms, however, relate to the methodologies used, but everyone will agree as to the importance of the Hawthorne Investigations in contributing to the understanding of socio-psychological factors affecting employee's behaviour at work.

"The Hawthorne Experiment began as a study into physical conditions and productivity. It ended as a series of studies into social factors: membership of groups, relationships with supervision etc. Its most significant findings showed that social relations at work were every bit as important as monetary incentives and good physical conditions. They also demonstrated the powerful influence of groups determining behaviour at work." [5]

Are the findings of the Hawthorne Experiments relevant today?

Most of the findings are taken for granted today. Social skills within the context of work are as important today as they were eight decades ago. Also, within the context of business complexity and increasing Globalisation, the Hawthorne Experiments remind us that employees are human beings and they **have needs and expectations**.

The study of the groups leading to the **study of teams** as we know today owes its origins to the Hawthorne Experiments. The Hawthorne Experiments drew our attention to the nature of the informal groups, and more importantly to the formation of group norms and the influence of these norms on human behaviour.

We know today that group formation and development incorporates four stages. They are:

- Forming;
- Storming;

---

5   Cole, G. A. (1986). 'Management Theory and Practice '. DP Publications. Pp47

- Norming; and

- Performing.

In **Forming**, stage members of the group explore the social relations and structure within the group. Members behave differently, some aggressively and some become passive in the exploration stage. At this stage the seeds of group integration and cohesion are being planted.

The **Storming** stage involves conflicts which result from the fact that members of the group get involved in asserting their roles according to their personalities, attitudes and their aspirations. At this stage all members get involved in jockeying for their positions in the group. Gradually they get rid of conflicts and begin to formulate group norms.

In the **Norming** stage, group values emerge and all members begin to accept a set of rules that will govern the way they will perform their roles. Group conformity emerges and, as a consequence, group sub-culture comes into existence.

The acceptance and the understanding of group sub-culture are very important from the point of view of organisational effectiveness. If this sub-culture is in tune with organisational culture then the group becomes very effective in achieving the organisational objectives set.

In the **performing stage**, the group cohesiveness has been developed and the behaviour of the group members is directed towards achieving objectives set for the task.

Understanding of group dynamics and group developmental stages is very important. Group cohesiveness does not come into existence over night. Many groups have been abandoned while at the storming stage because the 'management' felt that conflicts equal failure.

The effectiveness of any group depends on:

- structure;

- tasks;

- environment; and

- process.

Structure: the size and composition matter very much in group formation. In one utility industry the 'management' decided to form a group of 240 people. It failed to act as a group and no wonder! How can such a group manage its dynamics effectively? Composition of the group also plays a key role in its effectiveness. The global team would demand multi-national and multi-skills membership, whereas, in some situations, such multi-skills or mix of nationalities may not be necessary.

Tasks: Groups have to have objectives to provide necessary direction. Each task will demand different types of skills and personalities.

Environment: Group effectiveness depends on internal organisational environment such as its structure, management style, competencies and also external environment.

Process: Processes have to be put in place to accommodate the developmental stages of group formation. Facilitating free communication, providing adequate support and coaching, all play a key role in group success.

Such a focus on socio-psychological behaviour within the work situation has come about as consequences of the Hawthorne Experiments.

Group structure played a key role in the 1960s and 1970s in addressing 'ad hoc' business issues. They became 'quality circles' each consisting of about five to ten volunteers who worked under the supervisor, meeting once a week to identify and solve work-related problems. The growth rate of quality circles during the 1980s was phenomenal. It is estimated that in the early 1980s there were one million quality circles and ten million members.

The study of groups has led to the study of teams and team performance. Many experts make a distinction between groups and teams.

A group becomes a team when the following attributes are taken on board:

- *"There is a trust among team members.*

- *There is a common purpose and vision.*

- *Sacrifices in individuality are demanded.*

- *There is a discipline and guidance to what is acceptable and what is not acceptable.*

- *There is a specification of goals and associated performance indicators and measures.*

- *There is group accountability.*

- *There is sharing of experience, knowledge and communication.*

- *There is unrestricted interpersonal communication.*

- *There is commitment and involvement."* [6]

So, today, when we study teams and groups we must not forget the importance of social relations and the importance of workers' attitudes and behaviour, the factors which have been brought to our attention by the Hawthorne Experiments.

The other impact the experiments left us is the phenomenon of '**the Hawthorne Effect**'. This term is used to indicate the change in behaviour and morale of employees which result from management taking an interest in them. This effect should be considered whenever we conduct any investigation on human relations.

---

6 Kermally, S (1996). 'Total Management Thinking'. Butterworth-Heinemann. Pp 312.

Lessons learnt from Elton Mayo

- People like to feel important and have their work recognised.

- They like to be praised rather than blamed.

- They like to be consulted and be involved in decision-making.

- They have a sense of belonging and like to belong to a group. In a knowledge society they like to form and belong to communities of practice.

- Workers have a strong need to cooperate and communicate. organisations should capitalise on this need to create and share knowledge in order to win and sustain competitive advantage.

- A major preoccupation of management should be to develop and sustain cooperation. In modern jargon, management should provide counselling and coaching.

- Social skills are important for management in the knowledge era. According to Mayo, "Authority therefore, in actual exercise demands a capacity for vision and wise guidance that must be re-achieved daily; since the cooperation of others is a vital element in it, social understanding and social skills are involved equally with technological and capacity..."[7]

---

7   Elton Mayo (1945). 'The Social Problems of an Industrial Civilisation'. New Hampshire: Ayer. Pp 50.

FOUR
Abraham Maslow (1908-1970)

"What a man can be, he must be."

ABRAHAM MASLOW

Guru's profile

Abraham Maslow received his Ph.D. in Psychology in 1934/35 from the University of Wisconsin. His dissertation was on *The Role of Dominance in the Social and Sexual Behaviour of Infra-human Primates*. He lectured at Brooklyn College where he met many European intellectuals including Adler. He was on the faculty of Brooklyn College from 1937 to 1951. From 1951 he served as a chair of the psychology department at Brandeis University. He was there until 1961. After that he returned to California where he died of a heart attack in 1970.

Guru's contribution

Maslow published extensively throughout his professional life. He carried out a lot of studies on primates but after his Ph.D. he decided to focus his studies on human motivation.

In 1943 he published a paper, *A Theory of Human Motivation*, in which he put forward his needs theory which is known as 'Maslow's Hierarchy of Needs'. This theory, with some modification, is valid today in understanding human motivation and forms the basis of human motivation training. The theory has become the foundation of managing people. It provides insights for managers into what makes people tick and motivates them.

Maslow's hierarchy of needs in a nutshell

According to Maslow each of us is motivated by needs. These needs are innate. He presents these needs in a pyramid form consisting of five levels. He categorised these needs as physiological needs, safety needs, belonging and love, esteem needs and self-actualisation needs. These needs are further categorised as deficit needs and being needs.

The needs are hierarchically structured and they act as motivators. Their arrangement within the hierarchy depends on the urgency and priority to individuals.

"For the man who is extremely and dangerously hungry, no other interest exists but food. He dreams of food, he remembers food, he thinks about food, he emotes about food, he perceives only food, and he wants only food.....For our chronically and extremely hungry man, Utopia can be defined as a place where there is plenty of food. He intends to think that, if only he is guaranteed food for the rest of his life, he will be perfectly happy and will never want anything more. Life itself tends to be defined in terms of eating. Anything else will be defined as unimportant... Such a man may fairly be said to live by bread alone... But what happens to man's desires when there is plenty of bread and when his belly is chronically filled? At once other (and 'higher') needs emerge and these, rather than physiological hunger, dominate the organism." [8]

---

8 'A Theory of Human Motivation'. Psychological Review 50, pp 370-396.

Physiological needs

Air, food, drink, shelter, warmth and sex all come under physiological needs. All individuals have these needs and they have to be met. If unfulfilled then individuals would not be motivated to move up the hierarchy. Most of their activities will be confined to fulfilling these needs. These needs constitute the general well-being of individuals.

You can see many examples of people searching for physiological needs in some poor countries. The author was born in Zanzibar and he has experienced and witnessed poverty in many dimensions.

Safety needs

Once physiological needs are satisfied then safety needs become predominant. These needs reflect freedom from physical dangers.

The author is going through the second fatherhood. His three year old daughter behaves negatively if she feels she is in a threatening environment.

As far as individuals are concerned these needs relate to living in a safer environment, looking for job security, making provisions for pensions etc.

Belonging and love needs

These needs relate to the desire to belong in a group, family, organisation, relationship etc.

These needs focus on the social aspects of the work and non-work environment. In the Hawthorne Experiments, we noted the importance of social relationships within the group environment.

organisations provide coffee breaks, organise various forms of outings, social meetings etc. in order to accommodate these needs within the work environment. Interpersonal relations arise in work situations as a consequence of these needs.

Outside organisations we feel the need to form friendships, to belong to a club or social group, need to love and to be loved. The need for love is not the same as the need for sex. Fulfilment of sexual desires comes under the category of physiological needs. Love involves affectionate relationships with other people.

If we consider situations of expatriates and immigrants, we will observe that groups of immigrants and expatriates form their own communities in 'foreign' countries to satisfy security needs but also, most importantly, 'belonging needs'. They form their own clubs, their own neighbourhoods and so on.

Esteem needs

These needs relate to the need to feel good about ones self. An individual desires to master his or her own work. He or she wants to feel confident, adequate and capable. In a work situation if these needs are not met, an individual loses confidence in him or herself and assumes a sense of inferiority. When you constantly tell your staff they are useless they do become useless because they lose confidence and their self-esteem.

Wanting to be recognised and wanting to be respected constitute aspects of esteem needs.

Self-actualisation needs

"Even if all these needs are satisfied, we may still often (if not always) expect that new discontent and restlessness will soon develop, unless the individual is doing what he is fitted for. A musician must make music, an artist must paint, a poet must write, if he is to be ultimately happy. What a man can be, he must be. This need we may call self-actualisation." [9]

These needs reflect the desire to achieve one's potential. It is a complex drive which manifests in different forms in different individuals.

It is important to note that not all individuals possess these drives.

The type of people that had self-realisation and self-actualisation needs were people like Abraham Lincoln, Mahatma Ghandi and Albert Einstein. These types of people have the following characteristics:

- They have a clear perception of reality.

- They are problem-centred in that they treat problems as challenges which demand solutions.

- They are unique and value autonomy.

- They feel that the ends that one adopts do not necessarily justify the means.

- They rely on their own experiences and values.

- They possess compassion and humanity.

- They like to form intimate personal relations.

- They accept people as they are rather than as they would wish them to be.

- They are creative and original in their thinking.

---

9   A. H. Maslow 'A Theory of Human Motivation.' Psychological Review, Vol. 50 (1943). Pp370-396.

People who live in poverty or in an unsafe environment do not worry or think about self-realisation needs. They are focussed on achieving physiological and, more important, security needs.

Please Note: *"The need for self-realisation can impose upon the individual stronger bonds of self-discipline than could be enforced by someone else. It can make a person dissatisfied with his own performance when others praise it. Like other human needs of more basic priority, the drive for self-realisation can have pitfalls for the individual. In the extreme, it can become an obsession resulting in psychological or even physical self-destruction. At lesser levels of determination, it can make an individual difficult to work with for any prolonged interval. Frequently, it may lead to eccentric behaviour which others find alarming or annoying. Self-realisation as a drive can manifest itself in modes of behaviour which range from being a perfectionist to being power-hungry."* [10]

However, as human beings are perpetually wanting beings, all needs are never fully gratified.

According to Maslow these needs are arranged in a hierarchy of 'prepotency' that is in the urgency of the drive.

Over the years the classification of needs has been extended. However, the original version is used by many trainers in the field.

---

10 Fred J. Carvell (1970). 'Human Relations in Business'. The Macmillan Company. Pp71

Criticisms of Maslow's theory

Some researchers have not found the existence of a hierarchy of needs, although they do not argue that needs do exist.

In practice there is an overlap of needs. People are driven by many needs simultaneously. Maslow had not considered cultural differences that exist in human needs.

Some people have argued that when you consider what is happening in Afghanistan and Iraq now that people are fleeing away from their homes in order to find safety and to secure good future for themselves and their children.

In some cases some people like Rembrandt and Van Gogh went out of their way to meet self-actualisation needs while still struggling to meet physiological needs.

If one watches the development of children, they do strive for self-realisation needs as they develop. Maslow's concept of self-actualisation needs is very limited, applying to two percent of the population.

If you consider the case of Nelson Mandela, he was determined to achieve his self-actualisation needs in a situation where his security and belonging needs were not met.

In our modern climate job security has become a cause for concern. In this situation employees develop needs for security and self-actualisation concurrently.

A word of caution

In using Maslow's Hierarchy of Needs take care to consider the context of the situation you are dealing with. A friend of mine got his Business Management degree and was promoted to a manager of a well-known hotel and was sent to Mombassa, Kenya to manage a resort hotel there.

He applied the Hierarchy of Needs to motivate and recruit his staff. After offering what he thought to be a fair wage, he then decided to promote some of his staff and gave them uniforms and titles but without increasing their wages. He thought he would motivate them by accommodating their 'belonging needs'.

He was surprised when most of these promoted staff left him to go and do manual jobs elsewhere to increase their income. What he did not realise, is that for these staff what mattered most were physiological and security needs; making more money to look after their families. They left their villages to go to towns to earn money to feed their families.

Having learnt this lesson he got caught up again. He decided to increase their wages every year. In some cases, as individuals received more money some of them decided not to go to work and take some days off. In other words absenteeism increased. These people were willing to lose some of their income and instead enjoy leisure time. In this situation he could not see what he was doing wrong. He subsequently found out that some of his staff had the concept of 'target income' that is, once they received what they needed to maintain their families, they did not want to earn any more. In certain tribal sub-cultures this target income phenomenon existed.

It is very important, therefore, to understand the national cultural and individual differences before going all speed to apply Maslow's hierarchy.

Lessons learnt from Abraham Maslow

- If we disregard criticisms in relation to methodology and hierarchy, Maslow's theory has made a significant impact on those who have to manage people.

- He made us aware of different types of needs and this is as valid today as it was when he wrote about them.

- In this knowledge era we emphasise the need and the importance of knowledge sharing and knowledge creation. Employees would be willing to create and share knowledge if their needs are met. Knowledge workers need recognition and respect, and they also need to meet their self-actualisation needs. These needs may not be in a form of hierarchy but, nevertheless, these needs exist and they have been made aware to us by Maslow.

- We also talk about the 'communities of practice' within the context of knowledge management. One of the reasons for the formation of the communities of practice is the sense of belonging and recognition required by members of such communities.

- Maslow's theory also directs our attention to ask 'What happens if the needs are not met?' Within the organisational context, in order to manage people effectively, we have to consider the consequences of unmet needs and learn how to handle such situations. Unmet needs cause conflict and frustration and as a consequence the individuals involved do not give their best.

- Counselling and coaching techniques give us an insight into what makes people tick. We try to gain insights into their needs and behaviour and provide proper and adequate direction.

- In managing people today we should not reject his theory as being old or inappropriate. Like any other theory it has its usefulness if it is adapted to accommodate the changing context.

FIVE
Douglas McGregor (1906-1964)

"With every passing year, McGregor's message becomes ever more relevant, timelier and more important."

PETER DRUCKER

Guru's profile

Douglas McGregor was born in 1906 in Detroit, Michigan. He was one of the forefathers of contemporary management thinking. He got his degrees from Wayne State University and a Doctorate in Experimental Psychology from Harvard University. He joined Harvard University as a tutor in 1935 and in 1937 left to join MIT first as an instructor and then gaining professorship in 1948. From 1948 to 1954 he was the President of Antioch. He resigned from his presidency in 1954 to rejoin the MIT. He also undertook various consulting assignments in the areas of human and industrial relations.

Guru's contribution

In 1960 McGregor published his book 'The Human Side of Enterprise'[11], in which he put forward two sets of assumptions in relation to human behaviour. These sets of assumptions are presented as Theory X and Theory Y. Management has to use either set of needs to motivate people.

He grouped Maslow's five categories of needs into 'lower order' needs incorporating Physiological and Security Needs, and 'higher order' needs incorporating Belonging, Esteem and Self-actualisation Needs.

He accepts the point that man is a wanting animal. As soon as one of his needs is satisfied, another appears in its place. This process is unending. He, however, makes a point that a satisfied need is not a motivator of behaviour.

Like Maslow, his theory of motivation has had a significant impact in the field of managing people. He presented two approaches to managing people. The Theory X approach, with its associated assumptions, generally produces poor results and the Theory Y approach, with its associated assumptions, produces better perform-ance and results. **How managers manage people in practice depends on what assumptions they make about workers.** In a situ-ation where they make Theory X assumptions they will manage people by directing and controlling them, whereas in a situation where they make Theory Y assumptions they will manage people by involvement and by delegating responsibility.

So what are these basic assumptions made by managers?

---

11 Douglas McGregor (1960). 'The Human Side of Enterprise'. McGraw Hill.

Theory X approach and its assumptions

- People inherently dislike work. As a consequence, they have to be threatened (using disciplinary actions) before they work hard and also they have to be controlled.

- The average person prefers to be directed and is not keen on taking any responsibility. He or she is interested in focusing on meeting security needs.

He writes, *"Theory X explains the consequences of a particular managerial strategy; it neither explains nor describes human nature although it purports to. Because its assumptions are so unnecessarily limiting, it prevents our seeing the possibilities inherent in other managerial strategies. What sometimes appear to be new strategies – decentralisation, management by objectives, consultative supervision, 'democratic leadership' – are usually nothing but old wine in new bottles because the procedures developed to implement them are derived from the same inadequate assumptions about human nature. Management is constantly becoming disillusioned with widely touted and expertly merchandised 'new approaches' to the human side of enterprise. The real difficulty is that these new approaches are no more than different tactics – programs, procedures, gadgets – within an unchanged strategy based on Theory X."* [12]

Theory Y approach and its assumptions

- It is natural for human beings to put effort into work.

- Control and punishment are not the only ways to make people work.

---

12 D. S. Pugh (Ed) (1971). 'organisation Theory'. Penguin. Pp313.

- A person will direct himself or herself if they are committed to the organisational objectives and the job is satisfying.

- The average person will take responsibility if there were proper conditions.

- Employees like to use their imagination and creativity to make decisions to solve problems.

The use of the two approaches depends on the circumstances. In a situation where workers have to be controlled then the Theory X approach becomes appropriate. This might be the case, say on the shop floor.

In a situation where it is possible to get commitment from employees then the Theory Y approach is recommended. In such situations employees will assume self-direction and control to carry out their work.

However, McGregor wrote, *"Many statements have been made to the effect that we have acquired today the know-how to cope with virtually any technological problems which may arise, and that the major industrial advances of the next half century will occur on the human side of enterprise. Such advances, however, are improbable so long as management continues to organise and direct and control its human resources on the basis of assumptions – tacit or explicit – like those of Theory X. Genuine innovation, in contrast to a refurbishing and patching of present managerial strategies, requires first the acceptance of less limiting assumptions about the nature of the human resources we seek to control, and second the readiness to adapt selectively to the implications contained in those new assumptions. Theory Y is an invitation to innovation."*[13]

Some authors have referred to Theory X as an autocratic style of management and Theory Y as a participative style of management.

---

13 Ibid. pp323.

Autocratic managers like to take control and focus more on the task rather than the people. Their main objective is to get the job done.

Participative managers consult employees and involve them in making decisions.

It is generally believed that workers under Theory Y are far more prevalent in the work place than those under Theory X.

McGregor himself held the **'Pygmalion Effect'** view in that he felt if managers assumed workers to be lazy and treated them as such, then they would be lazy. On the other hand if they assumed that workers welcome challenges then they would respond accordingly.

These two approaches are now considered when examining the performance of school children. Teachers are discouraged from making assumptions that children are stupid and they need to be controlled and coerced. If they are treated with respect and involve them in the learning process they will achieve better results.

Criticisms of Theory X and Theory Y

It is not recommended to pigeon-hole people in the Theory X box or the Theory Y box. Researches have shown that what needs to be done is to fit people with the most appropriate jobs for them. If someone likes the job he is doing then he will perform well irrespective of the assumptions you make about him.

You cannot and should not apply one set of assumptions to fit all situations. Again, the focus should be on individual differences and needs.

There are groups of workers who would like to be directed and who are not keen on taking responsibility. Such workers would perform better under 'autocratic managers'.

Last thoughts on Theory Y and the Pygmalion Effect

"The term 'Pygmalion Effect' owes its origin to ancient Greek mythology, concerning a king of Cyprus, Pygmalion. The king, who was also an accomplished sculptor, once carved a beautiful figure of a woman in stone. He fell in love with his creation, and through the strength of his own will, aided by the grace of Venus, the Goddess of Love, brought the statue to life. (For those who feel cheated when a story is not completed, the king married her and lived happily ever after.)

George Bernard Shaw's play Pygmalion is also based on this concept. Professor Henry Higgins's confidence that he can convert a flower girl into a personable society lady who can pass off for a duchess, eventually transforms Eliza Doolittle. Without belittling Prof Higgins's skills as an expert on languages and dialects, Shaw attributed Eliza's transformation to his infectious enthusiasm and conviction of success. The Pygmalion effect has been tested repeatedly in different conditions and among different people, and has been found to be true. In factory settings, where poor performers were transferred from one place of work to another, and introduced as 'above average performers' to the new supervisor, remarkable results ensued. Not only did they outperform the average employee, but they were also assessed by peers as the most sought after team-members." [14]

Note: the expectation of a result most often leads to that result actually being achieved.

---

14 V. S. Mahesh (1993). *'Thresholds of Motivation'*. Tata-McGraw-Hill Publishing. Pp64

Lessons learnt from Douglas McGregor

- Using Theory X assumptions to manage people generally leads to workers being dissatisfied.

- Using Theory Y assumptions, on the other hand, leads to job satisfaction.

- It is important to gain commitment from employees in order to achieve organisational objectives and gain better performance.

- Control, coercion and control are not appropriate means of gaining commitment.

- Assumptions about human nature and behaviour influence the way we treat workers.

- In a knowledge era it is imperative for management to create a thriving work environment to facilitate the creation, sharing, using and reusing of knowledge. This requires management to focus on Theory Y assumptions.

- In their book *Douglas McGregor on Management – Revisiting the Human Side of Enterprise*,[15] Heil, Stephens and Bennis argue that McGregor's ideas are more important and relevant today than ever before. The book contains numerous examples of companies and leaders who have flourished under McGregor's approach.

---

15 Heil, G., Stephens, Deborah.C., Bennis, *Warren G (2000). 'Douglas McGregor Revisited – Managing the Human Side of the Enterprise*. John Wiley & Sons.

SIX
Frederick Herzberg (1923-)

"Take me the way I am, not the way
you want me to be."

FREDERICK HERZBERG

Guru's profile

Frederick Herzberg was a practising manager as well as an academic.
He was a professor of management and originator of the motivation-
hygiene theory. He was born in 1923 and is considered the father of
the job enrichment principle. He received his degrees from City College,
New York in 1946 and his Ph.D. from the University of Pittsburgh in
1950. He worked as a Research Director for Psychological Services
of Pittsburgh for six years and in 1957 he became professor of psychology at Case Western Reserve University in Cleveland. In 1972 he
became a distinguished professor of management at the University
of Utah.

Herzberg also undertook consulting work with government and
industry.

Guru's contribution

He became famous for his Motivation-Hygiene Theory which he published in his book *The Motivation to Work*[16] in 1959.

He and his associates conducted surveys and interviewed accountants and engineers to find out what factors made them like their work and what made them dislike their work.

He asked interviewees to respond to the following question: *"Think of the time when you felt exceptionally good or exceptionally bad about your job, either you're present job or any other job you have had.....Tell me what happened."*[17]

Those who liked their work attributed this situation to achievement, recognition, the nature of the work, responsibility and advancement. These were the factors related to **job content** and they led to higher motivation for the worker. These factors addressed higher level needs. Those who disliked their work and were dissatisfied cited company policy and administration, supervisor's lack of competence and poor working conditions – all these factors related to **job context**. From this he formulated his now famous motivational theory.

According to Herzberg there are two types of factors in motivation. There are those factors which if present will enhance performance and increase motivation. Then there are other factors which if they are absent will decrease motivation and have an unfavourable impact on performance. The first group of factors he calls motivating factors and the second group of factors he calls hygiene factors.

Note: the opposite of job satisfaction is the lack of job satisfaction, and not job dissatisfaction. The opposite of job dissatisfaction is an absence of dissatisfaction.

---

16 Frederick Herzberg (1959). 'The Motivation to Work.' John Wiley.

17 Frederick Herzberg, Bernard Mauser, Barbara B. Snyderman (1959), 'The Motivation to Work'. John Wiley.

"We normally think of satisfaction and dissatisfaction as opposites; i.e. what is not satisfying must be dissatisfying, and vice versa. But when it comes to understanding the behaviour of people in their jobs, more than a play on words is involved."[18]

What are hygiene factors?

These factors which promote work satisfaction include a clean and safe environment, working conditions, supervision and money. If working conditions are poor, if a situation is unsafe or if there is poor supervision then they will lead to dissatisfaction and poor performance.

The hygiene factors relate to a work environment. An appropriate working environment provides workers with physiological, security and belonging needs, as explained in Maslow's theory of the Hierarchy of Needs. It provides basic needs, adequate security, a sense of belonging and comradeship.

What are motivators?

These factors include a sense of achievement, advancement, job interest, recognition and responsibility. These factors are the true motivators.

According to Herzberg, hygiene factors have to be attended to first before motivators start to work.

The uniqueness of his theory relates to the fact that he put forward different factors for satisfaction and dissatisfaction.

---

18 Frederick Herzberg . 'One More Time: How do you Motivate Employees?'. HBR January, 2003. pp91

Management should motivate people by paying attention to motivators. Hygiene factors have to reach a certain level first, to make sure motivation is not decreased, but after that focus should be put on motivating factors. Many managers, according to him, attempt to motivate through hygiene factors alone which is wrong and ineffective.

Application of Herzberg's theory

"In practice, numerous firms have applied these notions and report improvements in other measures of organisational performance. To illustrate, the results of just three firms, perhaps the best publicised ones, will be summarised [19]. Texas Instruments has a 'plan-do-control' program for workers, which has reduced costly overtime, freed the supervisors from close supervision, and enabled the company to increase productivity. In American Telephone and Telegraph, a job enrichment program applied to nine workers with no supervisory jobs, reduced the employee turnover rate in those jobs 13 percent and improved quality of performance, quantity of work, and customer services. Imperial Chemical Industries (Great Britain) declares that it has been able to save over $200,000 per year by adopting a job enrichment program. In each of these instances as a result of Herzberg and his associates."[20]

Herzberg's theory means that if you give someone more pay or a new title (hygiene factors) without extra responsibilities, it will stop him complaining about the job but it will not motivate him to do more work. Employees should be motivated by the job and through the use of the carrot and stick.

---

19 For further information on Texas Instruments, see M. Scott Myers. '*Every Employee a Manager*'. New York; McGraw-Hill Book co. 1970; for A.T. & T. see Robert H. ford, '*Motivation Through Work Itself*', New York American Management Associations 1969; and for Imperial Chemical Industries, see W. Paul, I Robertson and F. Herzberg, '*Job Enrichment Pays off*', HBR, Vol 47 (1969)pp61-79.

20 Daniel A. Wren, Dan Voich Jr (1968). '*Management – Process Structure and Behaviour*'. John Wiley. Pp457.

Herzberg's theory also contributed to the policy of 'Job Enrichment'. What job enrichment does is introduce a worker's responsibility for the job he is doing, thus promoting his interest in the job.

"In attempting to enrich certain jobs, management often reduces the personal contribution of employees rather than giving them opportunities for growth in their accustomed jobs. Such endeavours, which I shall call horizontal loading (as opposed to vertical loading or providing motivator factors), have been the problem of earlier job enlargement programs. Job loading merely enlarges the meaningless of the job.

The principles of vertical loading have not all been worked out as yet, but I have furnished seven useful starting points for consideration.

These are:

- *Removing some controls while retaining accountability.*

- *Increasing the accountability of individuals for their own work.*

- *Giving a person a complete natural unit of work (module, division, area, and so on).*

- *Granting additional authority to employees in their activity; job esteem.*

- *Making periodic reports directly available to the workers themselves rather than to supervisors.*

- *Introducing new and more difficult tasks not previously handled.*

- *Assigning individuals specific or specialised tasks, enabling them to become experts."* [21]

---

21 Frederick Herzberg. 'One More Time: How do you Motivate Employees'. HBR January, 2003. pp93.

Criticisms of Herzberg's theory

1   Only engineers and accountants were interviewed. These findings may not apply to other professional groups.

2   His methodology for conducting research led to such findings.

3   His methodology also lacked scientific rigour.

4   Hygiene factors and motivators vary depending on the types of individuals involved and the nature of the work examined.

5   Some argue that both job context and content produce satisfiers and dissatisfiers.

6   There is no evidence to prove that highly satisfied people are also high performers.

7   *"The Herzberg theory, or two-factor theory of motivation or Motivator-Hygiene M-H) theory, has given rise to a mass of investigations and experiments in industry and in many different types of organisations. Results do not always support Herzberg; in fact, only about one in three do so. Donald Hebb once said that when it is a question of survival, theories are like women – fecundity is more important than purity. M-H theory has certainly been very fertile – more so perhaps than any other theory in applied social psychology. Many industrial psychologists have not only survived but indeed thrived on the theory. The fecundity of the theory is not in doubt but its purity certainly is highly suspect."*[22]

---

22 Godfrey Gardner. *'Is there a valid test of Herzberg's two-factor theory?'*. J. Occupational Psychology, 1977, 50, pp197.

However, according to Donald D. White of the University of Arkansas, *"In the most comprehensive review of the literature on Herzberg's work, Bockman (1971) concluded that critics' objections to Herzberg's theory and/or his method, often have been made with complete disregard for the explanations Herzberg himself presented. She suggests that those who refute Herzberg are in fact measuring something other than what he studied. She goes so far as to suggest that many of those who have attempted to debunk Herzberg did so with the intent of gaining a reputation for 'gunning him down'. Although Bockman's research review concluded that there was considerable support for the two-factor theory, numerous researchers have continued to address themselves to the methods, hypotheses and applicability of the theory."*[23]

There is no doubt Herzberg's theory has been both influential and controversial.

Lessons learnt from Frederick Herzberg

- Focusing on hygienic factors to motivate employees will not work.

- Provide people with opportunities for responsibility, achievement and personal growth because this is the same as enabling people to achieve their self-actualisation needs.

- Redesign jobs to make work meaningful to people.

- Individuals with strong growth needs respond positively to enrich jobs.

- Individuals can be both very satisfied and very dissatisfied at the same time.

---

23 Donald D. White. 'The Two-Factor Theory: New Questions, New Answers.' This project was financed by a grant from the University of Arkansas Foundation Inc.

- Knowledge workers will respond more to sharing and creating organisational knowledge if they are motivated by high–order needs.

- Empowerment is about enriching jobs, allowing individuals to achieve higher levels needs.

SEVEN

Victor Vroom (1932-)

"If a worker sees high productivity as a path leading to the attainment of one or more of his (or her) personal goals, he (or she) will tend to be a high producer."

VICTOR VROOM

Guru's profile

Victor Vroom is John G. Searle Professor of organisation and Management. He gained his degrees from McGill University during the period 1953-1955 and his Ph.D. from the University of Michigan. He has gained various achievements and honours. His book *Work and Motivation* (1964) is regarded as a landmark in that field. Apart from his academic work Professor Vroom has undertaken various consultancy assignments with major corporations.

Guru's contribution

From the late 1960s the focus changed from needs theories of motivation to examining HOW people are motivated and what sustains motivation.

Under the umbrella of expectancy theories some management theorists put forward the view that whether a person is motivated or not depends on his perception of the outcome of his effort. If the outcome meets his needs then he will be motivated. There has to be a link between effort and performance (his expectancy) for him to be motivated.

Vroom's expectancy theory

Vroom's expectancy theory explains that when employees are given choices they choose the option that promises to give them the greatest reward.

Employees generally ask three questions to motivate themselves:

1. Can I do what I am being asked to do?

2. Would I be rewarded for doing it?

3. Do I want the reward on offer?

There are three basic elements of his expectancy theory:

1 expectancy;

2 instrumentality; and

3 valence.

Expectancy

This is an individual's belief that by making a great deal of effort, he will accomplish a lot. An individual's expectancy in relation to the effort plays a key part in his behaviour.

If an individual feels that no matter how hard he works the company will not pay any attention, he will not make much effort.

This belief or perception, is generally based on an individual's past experience, self-confidence, or the difficulty of achieving set goals.

An individual's perception is affected by his belief that he can perform the task well, by the goals set, and the control he exercises in his job.

Instrumentality

Even if an individual works hard if his efforts are not going to be awarded, (for example, if he feels he is now at the top of the salary scale) there is going to be a lack of motivation.

The instrumentality is the belief that if he works hard the outcomes will earn him reward which can be in a form of salary increase or promotion, or some form of recognition.

Instrumentality depends on trust and company policies.

For example, a senior manager at one of the leading consultancy companies was often promised directorship if she increased her billable hours. Unfortunately for her this promise was never kept. As a consequence she lost trust in her boss and in the organisation.

Valence

This simply refers to the value an individual places on an event or outcome. Even if an employee believes that his contribution will lead to an improvement in the company's performance and that his award will be commensurate with his effort and contribution, he will be poorly motivated if those rewards have a low valence to him. It is the value that this individual attaches to the outcome that matters.

For example, a telesales person's expectancy is his or her belief that the more calls he/she makes the more sales will materialise. If he/she feels that more sales will not materialise then he/she will not make more effort. His/her instrumentality is that higher sales will earn him/her more commissions. His/her valence is the importance he/she attaches to these commissions.

Criticisms of Vroom's theory

1 Research evidence so far has not supported the expectancy theory.

2 It is a very complicated theory.

3 In many work situations individuals do not have choices.

4 It is difficult to find out how much value is attributed to various outcomes.

5 It reduces motivation to a logical analysis of value and expectation.

Expectancy theory and managing people today

In today's environment the fundamental question an employee asks is, 'What's in it for me?' The answer that will motivate and satisfy an individual will depend on:

- what the organisation expects of an individual;

- what an individual expects of an organisation;

- what the employees value; and

- whether the employees' values are congruent with the organisation values.

Lessons learnt from Victor Vroom

- Define what you expect from your employees.

- Consider your employees' goals and structure work to facilitate achievement of these goals.

- Set objectives realistically and clearly.

- Set measurable and meaningful objectives.

- Coach your employees to be able to achieve the goals set.

- Provide adequate support for success.

- Set a realistic and meaningful appraisal system.

- Clarify the link between performance and reward.

- There is no point in offering rewards which employees do not value.

- Provide rewards for success.

EIGHT
Chris Argyris (1923-)

"…human beings come into organisations programmed to create intricate networks and layers of organisational defences that become self-reinforcing and self-proliferating."

CHRIS ARGYRIS

Guru's profile

Chris Argyris is the James Bryant Conant Professor Emeritus of Education and organisational Behaviour at Harvard University. He was born in July, 1923 in Newark, New Jersey. He got his first degree in Psychology from Clark and Kansas University and his doctorate in organisational Behaviour from Cornell in 1951. He has also received honorary doctorates from McGill University, University of Leuven and Stockholm School of Economics. He has published extensively on numerous subjects including those on organisational learning, leadership and communication. In this chapter we will focus on his contribution in the area of motivation.

Apart from his academic work, he also consults with many international organisations and various government departments.

Guru's contribution

Argyris believes that some organisations block the basic human need to express oneself and to do work successfully. Such a situation does not promote employee motivation and results in poor performance.

During the period of the 1950s and 1960s Argyris focused his attention on the relationships between individuals and organisations. *"Argyris feels that some organisational and managerial practices (for example, highly specialised jobs and narrow span of management) keep people from moving toward maturity. Since people want to develop mature personalities, negative human reactions may result: (1) persons may leave the organisation; (2) they may climb the organisational ladder to achieve more autonomy; (3) they may daydream, become aggressive, regress (that is, return to more infantile forms of behaviour), or use other defence mechanisms; (4) they may become apathetic or non-involved; and (5) they may create and formalise informal groups to sanction their own apathy, disinterest, restriction of output, aggression, and so on. Management faced with these reactions, may react by becoming more autocratic and by tightening organisational controls."* [24]

He put forward a theory which suggests that people tend to behave like Theory X behaviour mainly because it is not that they are lazy but in practice organisations treat them like immature individuals. This led to his Immaturity-Maturity Theory.

According to this theory human personality develops from immaturity to maturity in a continuum in which a number of key changes take place. These are as follows:

Immaturity	Maturity
Passivity	Activity
Dependence	Relative independence

---

24 Daniel A. Wren and Dan Voich, Jr. (1968). *'Management: Process, Structure, and behaviour'*. John Wiley. Pp395-396.

Behave in few ways	Behave in many ways
Erratic, shallow interest	Deeper interests
Short term perspective	Long term perspective
Subordinate position	Equal or superior position
Lack of awareness of self	Awareness and control over self

According to Argyris, many organisations still adhere to a bureaucratic/pyramidal value system. This type of system leads to mistrust within organisations and workers are not recognised as mature individuals.

In order to enable individuals to exhibit traits of maturity the organisation has to assume a humanistic/democratic value system. In this type of environment individuals will develop trusting relationships and they will be motivated to put in the effort to enhance organisational effectiveness. The organisation will become an exciting place to work in.

Defensive routines

Argyris put forward a concept of 'defensive routines'. They are thoughts and actions 'which protect individuals and organisations' in ways of dealing with reality. They are used to reduce pain and according to Argyris they can cause failures when used counter productively. They can also block learning in organisations.

Counterproductive defensive routines exhibit themselves in inflexible thinking and they also arise as a result of subordinates experiencing intolerable bosses.

Consider this

The head of one of the global training companies, based in Brussels was an autocratic leader and he led by fear and intimidation. The motto among the staff was 'keep your nose clean and head down'. Everyone made the effort to achieve the organisational objectives because they wanted to be in their jobs but no one made extra effort to increase organisational effectiveness. This is what defensive routines are all about – they create a special mindset to deal with such situations.

Argyris with Schon[25] put forward 'Theories of action: theory in use and espoused theory.'

They argue that people have mental maps with regard to how they act in different situations. These maps influence their behaviour and their actions. Not many people are aware of the existence of such maps. What they espouse is different to what they do.

When a person is asked as to how he would behave in certain circumstances, his answer is influenced by his espoused theory. However, how he behaves is influenced by his theory in action. Personal effectiveness and organisational effectiveness are achieved if there is congruence between these theories. In the absence of such congruence effective learning, either at individual level or organisational level, does not take place.

One needs to consider the use of defensive routines within the context of the nature of organisations. Argyris presents two models of organisations; they are Model I. and the other one is Model II.

---

25 Argyris, C and Schon, D. (1974). *'Theory in Practice: Increasing professional effectiveness.* Jossey Bass.

The Model I organisation has the following characteristics:

In Model I the organisations employees will deploy defensive routines. Employees within the context of the Model I culture will often say one thing while believing another. The theory espoused is at variance with the theory in use. When employees express their views within this context, they say what they think others want to hear.

In the Model II context employees feel safe and secured. In such an organisation employees are motivated to create and share knowledge. They are honest and open and they are not afraid to tell the truth.

As Argyris says, *"There is nothing particularly new about Model II as an espoused theory of action. The challenge is to transform it into a theory in use. Acquiring Model II as a theory of use does not mean that we should discard Model I. The latter is more effective for routine no threatening issues. The former is more effective for no routine, innovative issues as well as those that are threatening and valid descriptions of reality by those of us with contradictory views."*[26]

According to Argyris, we do not manage people as such. We manage the knowledge that they carry. To facilitate collaboration and bring about innovations, leaders have to create model II organisations.

Criticisms of Argyris's theory

- It is very academic.

- It is very complicated for practising managers to understand.

- It is very difficult to put his ideas into practice.

- It is difficult to see how his concepts can be used to manage people.

---

26 Chris Argyris (1985). *'Strategy, Change and Defensive Routines'*. Pitman. Pp261-262.

Chris Argyris's theory provides us with an insight into the importance of the mental maps employees hold and how the nature of organisations can trigger off the use of such maps.

To manage people effectively one has to understand the inter-relationship between the organisation and its people, and the existence of metal maps in order to achieve organisational effectiveness.

The HR.Com editor interviewed Robert Putnam, a colleague of Professor Chris Argyris. **This interview reflects how one can use Argyris's ideas in practice**. It is reproduced here with kind permission of the editor.

··

Interview: Robert Putnam, applying Argyris

David Creelman

A long-time colleague of Harvard professor Dr. Chris Argyris, Robert Putnam, makes his living applying these ideas.

David Creelman spoke to Dr. Putnam about putting academic insights into practice.

DC- Can you give me a little background on how you met Dr. Argyris?

RP- I took a doctoral program at Harvard and was very drawn to Chris, his work and his way of working with those of us in the class. I did my dissertation with him, and co-wrote Action Science with Dr. Argyris and Diana McLain Smith. That was a career forming experience and our practice has grown from that foundation.

DC- As you've moved into practice, which of Dr. Argyris' ideas have you embraced?

RP- One of the first things Chris ever said to us is that people design action to achieve intended consequences. If you help them understand the nature of the design you'd have a very powerful lever for helping people improve their effectiveness. That was the starting point for applying Chris' ideas. We called ourselves 'Action Design' with the notion of helping people recognise and talk about the designs that implicitly inform their action.

We also use the tool concepts that have become quite popular such as advocacy, inquiry, the ladder of inference, the left-hand column, and so on.

DC- I'm interested in starting with the more concrete artefacts. Most of our readers are likely to have come across these ideas.

RP- Let me start with the 'left-hand column' tool. We ask people to write a dialogue case of an important episode that illustrates the kind of interaction they would like to handle more effectively. You take a piece of paper, draw a line down the middle and on the right you write down what was actually said, as near as you can remember, and in the left-hand column you write any unspoken thoughts or feelings you had during the conversation. So when we speak of the left-hand column it refers to your unspoken thoughts or feelings when you are in the midst of a difficult interaction.

DC- What do people get out of this exercise?

RP- People find it helpful just to write down the cases because it enables them to look at one of these difficult interactions and to see the nitty-gritty of how it happened. When you review what you've written you get insights into what you did and didn't do.

It's also a very good basis for a professional development session because it gives us the opportunity to take a look at how you acted in the moment, what the other person did to trigger you, and how you were thinking at that time. People find all these unexpected puzzles and interesting anomalies when they look at what they were thinking that led them to say this but not say that, and how the other person misunderstood. It gives people a good insight into their own thinking and behaviour that may contribute to not getting the results they want.

DC- This brings me to one of my central questions about Chris Argyris' work. They sound like great ideas and I have seen them successfully employed in training programs, but it's rare to see them spontaneously used in the workplace.

RP- The learning process to develop the skill to interact more effectively requires ongoing attention. A one-shot training program cannot possibly be more than a beginning. So the question of sustaining practice over time, so that you really develop significant new skills, is a very important one.

With the left-hand column in particular, we find that within minutes people begin saying things like, "Let me tell you my left-hand column on that one." So it very quickly provides a language for people to voice things they would not otherwise have said.

That's the upside but there are limits too. There is a reason things stay on people's left-hand columns – saying them might create problems. Handling this requires developing two kinds of skill: saying difficult things and responding to the reactions others have in productive ways and, even more fundamentally, learning to think differently in the first place so that what appears on your left-hand column can be said. Developing these abilities takes time and practice. As Chris often said, it takes about as much practice as learning to play tennis.

DC- The ladder of inference is another Argyris tool that really appeals to me but I haven't seen it used much in practice.

RP- The ladder of inference is a simple model of how the human mind works in everyday life. The world is full of all kinds of data, far more than the human mind can pay attention to. The bottom rung of the ladder of inference is the data you've chosen to notice. Then you go through an interpretation process that assigns meaning to that selected data, which takes us to the second rung. That interpretation leads to a conclusion, the third rung that may lead you to take some action.

So in its simplest form the ladder of inference has three steps: the selected data, the interpretation steps in your inference process, and your conclusion at the top. These steps occur at the speed of thought, so fast that we're usually not consciously aware of the steps in our reasoning process. To an important degree our reasoning is a secret from ourselves. The ladder of inference becomes useful in helping people recognise when both they and others have jumped through several inferential steps to draw a conclusion. They are disagreeing about the conclusion, and what they need to do to make progress is make explicit the data they have selected and the steps in their interpretation process.

DC- How have you seen this put into practice?

RP- I've seen it used in all kinds of conversations and meetings I facilitate. One of my current clients has invested in leadership development for their senior team and has learned these tools. I'm helping them embed the skills in their day-to-day work. In the course of their conversations they will say things like, "Hold on, Jack. I think you are jumping the ladder of inference on that one." Or they will say, "I know I'm jumping up the ladder on this." That creates an opportunity for them to walk through the data and interpretations that led to the conclusion.

DC- That's encouraging. Why is it so rare to bump into people talking this way and using these tools?

RP- The problem is that the tools are so conceptually straightforward and so easy to stick into a training program that in minutes somebody will say, "Oh, I understand that." They think they've got it but the tools are profoundly difficult to put into practice in the heat of the moment. I've been in organisations where they've trained hundreds or thousands of people in these tools and ironically it's almost as if they've inoculated the organisation against the deep learning the tools can provide. People think, "We've already done that."

Over the years we've discovered that giving everyone brief training, even when it starts with top management, is not a good approach. People do the workshops, find the tools easy to understand, and assume that good intentions are all it takes to use them. But they look around and see that their boss, who had the same program, still gets frustrated and in the heat of the moment makes the same imperious, unilateral moves they have learned to hate. Then they say, "See, the stuff doesn't work," or "the top is not using it," and it falls into disuse.

The strategy that does make a profound difference is to have a small number of people who make a much larger commitment to learning to use the tools in practice. Then you get the genuine behaviour change even under a significant degree of stress. That's when you begin to see sustainable change.

DC – This is a critical idea for HR managers. The normal approach is to train all our managers about one concept or another without any of them truly becoming particularly proficient. It's a very appealing approach but it is probably a foolish strategy. It's like the idea that it'd be nice if all your managers understood finance but frankly what the corporation really needs is a few people deeply steeped in finance, not a bunch of dilettantes.

Maybe for these tools we are better off developing a few specialists and bringing them in when they are needed—just like we call in the finance pros when we need them. That might be a better investment than buying 5,000 copies of the book and wondering why nothing changes.

RP- You've described two extremes, the brief training for 5,000 versus the deep expert. I think it is very helpful to have a few deep experts, but I would also say there is a mid-range that is very important. To use your finance analogy you want some of your key managers, especially at senior levels, to have a pretty good working knowledge of finance. It's that mid-level of skill between the very limited understanding and the true specialist that I would like to see more of.

We have found the way to achieve this is by working with people on real issues. As they begin to interact differently and see that contributing to progress on their business issue, they incorporate the skills into their normal behaviour. Others in the organisation see that, and you begin to get traction.

DC- Of all the ideas you use in your consulting, are there one or two that are particularly powerful?

RP- The concept of framing and re-framing has great power. What we mean by framing is the way in which people define a situation, how they construct their role and their view of other people in the situation. For example, if there is a problem with a new employee someone might immediately frame it as a hiring mistake whereas someone else might frame it as an orientation issue. Typically we frame things spontaneously without thinking about it. The frame just presents itself to you as an objective reality. However, it's not an objective reality; it's a construction of the human mind influenced by the culture we are in. The way we frame a situation channels what actions appear relevant to us.

In our professional development work we help people make that frame explicit so that it becomes possible to think how you might want to re-frame it, how you might think differently about the situation and redefine what you're trying to achieve. This opens up more powerful options.

DC- The idea of framing is one concept that may have entered the general consciousness of business. It wouldn't surprise me to be in a meeting and hear someone say, "Let's reframe this," and actually use the concept in the correct way. For example, something might originally be framed as a marketing issue and someone will say, "No, we need to re-frame this, it's a product development issue."

RP- That's a useful observation because it points to the distinction between technical or business issues and the behavioural realm. When it comes to behaviour and interaction, people have enormous difficulty changing their frames. A client of mine is in the pharmaceutical industry. The research division and the marketing division have entrenched views of each other. Researchers see marketers as having a set of characteristics; marketers see researchers as having other characteristics, and those views are very persistent. And they lead each group to dismiss the validity or legitimacy of what the other says, and to treat that as undiscussable. Getting those departments to work better together will require each of them to do some reframing. I was working with one of those groups recently and we identified their current frame. Then I asked, "What might be a way of reframing it?" They drew a blank. The leader said, "I think we'll need help to see another framing."

DC- Is there anything you disagree with Dr. Argyris about?

RP- One of the ways our differences show up is how my partners and I think about and help people work on key relationships. organisational issues can get bound up in what we call relationship structures that form between particular individuals. Helping people change those structures requires a shift of focus from Chris' construct of Model I and Model II.

DC- As I understand it, Model I is our normal mode of thinking where we, among other things, try to appear rational and in control while suppressing negative feelings. Whereas Model II is a mode of thinking that stresses getting valid information, making informed choices and constantly monitoring to be sure we are on track and being honest with ourselves.

RP- In our work we call them the unilateral action model and the mutual action model. By cutting the world in this bi-polar way you simplify things enormously, you create the sense that everyone is in the same boat, and you highlight the impact on learning. On the other hand it glosses over differences that become important when you are trying to help people see how they trigger each other.

DC- One of our readers wondered if there are any programs to help young people reach Model II before they join the workforce.

RP- In the '70s when Chris moved from Yale to Harvard he had a co-appointment in the Business School and the School of Education, where he was when we worked with him. He thought if you could change school systems, and therefore educate young people in Model II, you could really change the world. Unfortunately he found the education system impenetrable. It was enormously difficult to get traction with school system administrators and faculty. The business world was much more receptive to him. There are people working with these ideas in schools but I'm not close to it, and I don't know of programs to help young people learn Model II.

Now speaking personally as the father of a 15-year-old son I think Model 1 is a capability you need to develop as you're growing up. However, I also believe, based on my sample of Model I, that some of the key Model II capabilities of reflecting on your own thinking and having increased awareness that other people may think differently can be developed at a young age.

DC- Another reader felt that Chris Argyris criticisms of employee empowerment have really condemned the concept. Is that fair?

RP- I think what Chris condemns is the charade of empowerment because it gets used so widely as an espoused theory when it just isn't so. Many change programs say they empower people when they do not. So this talk of empowerment actually generates cynicism. I think Chris is all for empowerment when it is genuinely possible, but to be real about it we also have to own up to the limits to what is possible.

DC- There are a lot of people who are real Argyris enthusiasts, but many of them find it frustrating that the world hasn't made more progress in adopting his ideas. I think that's one of the under-

lying concerns of all the people who have discussed his work with me.

RP- In Allen Ginsburg's poem *The Terms in Which I Think of Reality* one passage reads, "*For the world is a mountain of shit: if it's going to be moved at all, it's got to be taken by handfuls.*" I actually find that hopeful. The world is a big complex difficult place, and there are all these highly intelligent people wanting to make things happen and afflicted with all the blind spots of the human race. If you look at the social cognition literature it shows that people are overconfident in their own judgments and convinced of the purity of their own intentions while attributing bad motives to other people. People look for confirming data and don't notice disconfirming data. It creates a lot of crossed wires, a lot of impatience and frustration. So it's really a matter of moving it by handfuls or, to change the metaphor, bailing while the water keeps coming in.

. . . .

Robert Putnam and his colleagues in Action Design offer a five-day professional development workshop, 'Creating Productive Conversations', that helps practitioners develop the skills in using the ideas discussed here. Information is on their web site at www.actiondesign.com.

Lessons learnt from Chris Argyris

- Promote honesty within your organisation.

- Be honest with yourself and open up to your shortcomings and failures.

- Motivate people by creating collaborative corporate culture.

- Reward openness.

- Consider not only the needs and the psychology of the individual but the culture of the company in motivating people to enhance organisational effectiveness.

- By your leadership and example promote congruence between theory espoused and theory in use.

NINE
John Adair (1934-)

"Good leaders today will tend to see people as colleagues, companions or partners, not followers. As one progresses through levels of leadership, of course, many of those colleagues will be leaders in their own right."

JOHN ADAIR

Guru's profile

John Adair was born in 1934. He holds higher degrees from the Universities of Oxford and London. He was a senior lecturer in Military History and Leadership Training Advisor at the Royal Military Academy, Sandhurst. After two years as the first Director of Studies at St. George's House in Windsor Castle he became Associate Director of the Industrial Society where he pioneered Action-Centered Leadership.

In 1979 he became the world's first Professor of Leadership Studies at the University of Surrey, and is currently Visiting Professor at the University of Exeter.

He now works as an international consultant in leadership and management development.

Guru's contribution

He pioneered the **Action-Centered Leadership** approach.

John Adair found that effective leaders paid attention to three areas of management. They are task, team (or the group) and individual. These three areas are interdependent.

Task needs involve setting clear goals and objectives

Team needs involve interaction, support, communication and shared work.

Individual needs incorporate personal behaviour and feelings. These vary amongst individuals.

People expect their leaders to provide support and help them to build synergy of teamwork and to attend to individual needs.

"The Task, Team and Individual needs overlap. To achieve the common task, maintain network and satisfy the individuals, certain functions have to be performed. These functions (the functional approach to leadership also called action-centered leadership) are:

- *Defining the task*

- *Planning*

- *Briefing*

- *Controlling*

- *Evaluating*

- *Motivating*

- *Organising*

- *Providing an example.*

These leadership functions need to be handled with excellence and this is achieved by performing those functions with increasing skill.

Leaders need to exhibit the following attributes/qualities/characteristics in exercising the functions:

1. GROUP INFLUENCE

To generate a group willingness to achieve a desired goal/objective.

2. COMMAND

To decide upon a course of action as quickly as the situation demands and to carry it through with a firmness and strength of purpose.

3. COOLNESS

To remain cool or unperturbed under testing or trying conditions.

4. JUDGEMENT

Ability to arrange available resources and information in a systematic and commonsense way to produce effective results.

5. APPLICATION/RESPONSIBILITY

To demonstrate sustained effort combined with a degree of dependability in order to complete a task or achieve an objective.

Having identified the main functions or principles of leadership, there are skills in providing those functions in different situations and managers need to develop their abilities to bring those skills to bear in increasing levels of excellence.

Two of the main strengths of Adair's concept are that it is timeless and is not culture or situation-dependent. For over three decades, the now familiar 'three circle' Action-Centered Leadership model has been integrated into company cultures, individual's leadership styles and is an established core competency hallmark of management and supervisory training doctrine in a great number of organisations. For many years, Adair's model has been taught in the civil service, public services and the armed forces, as well as in business schools, management colleges, and universities. Interestingly, HMS Excellent, the Royal Navy's

School of Leadership and Management has even incorporated the three circles into its official ship's badge.

A third strength of Action-Centered Leadership is that it can help the leader to identify where he, or she, may be operating out of kilter with the real needs of the group or situation. For example, over preoccupation with the bottom-line and end-result statistics and, therefore, inordinately high preoccupation with task needs may well mean that individuals and/or teams see their needs as being of relatively minor significance to the leader. Conversely, over-preoccupation with people's needs, trying always to please others and avoiding tough decisions which need to be made, can quickly lead to task avoidance, weak decision-making and poor results.

As the Chief Executive of a major pharmaceutical company puts it:

'X spends far too much time trying to please people, instead of getting on with what's really wanted. He tells me what he thinks I want to know and if he does that with me, he will do it with others. I can't trust him to deliver – he's too bothered about being nice to people, so that results often suffer in his area'.

Following a management programme, the Financial Director of a company manufacturing fasteners for the aerospace industry said:

'Those three circles help in that they bring home the need for me to try to keep things in balance. I can focus on one or two things at the expense of the other areas, but only for a short time, before the cracks begin to appear.'"[27]

---

27 Michael Williams. (1998). 'Mastering Leadership'. Thorogood. Pp33-35

Developing leadership skills

"organisations (and if you are the leader of one that means you) should ensure that they have a policy of developing the leadership potential in all and particularly of newly appointed 'leaders'. Individuals should also ensure that they focus on developing their leadership skills by training, reading, analysing and following the example of good leaders and by assessing, monitoring and improving their own performance." [28]

John Adair believes leadership is trainable. His work incorporates much of the thinking on human needs and motivation by Maslow and Herzberg.

The Adair Leadership Foundation

"The Foundation brings you the definitive approach to leadership development. Its proven models and practical methods have stood the test of time and produced impressive results. At the Adair Leadership Foundation we believe that investment in leadership is the key to success in any organisation, while at the same time developing your key asset-people.

Although John Adair's philosophy was conceived over 30 years ago, it has been continually improved to ensure it is still the best in the world. Its contribution to your organisation will ensure that you are competitive in today's challenging business environment." [29]

---

28 The above material is quoted from: 'The John Adair Handbook of Management and Leadership (1998), edited by Neil Thomas. Pp123-143

29 'The Adair Leadership Programme', Falconbury Ltd, London

Lessons learnt from John Adair

- Leadership is about giving direction, providing inspiration, building teams, setting examples and gaining acceptance.

- Sources of leadership power are position, personality and knowledge.

- An effective leader has to be enthusiastic, have integrity, be tough and fair, have humility and be confident.

- Three variables affecting leadership are the leader, the situation and the group.

- Leaders can be trained.

- Leadership is a transferable skill.

- One of the main results of good leadership is a good team.

TEN
Warren Bennis (1925-)

"Learning to be a leader is virtually the same process as becoming an integrated and healthy person."

WARREN BENNIS

Guru's profile

Warren Bennis is foremost an authority on organisational development, leadership and change. He is a University Professor and Distinguished Professor of Business Administration at the University of Southern California. He received his Ph.D. in Economics and Social Science at MIT and then taught at Sloan School of Management. He was the successor to Douglas McGregor as chairman of the organisation Studies department at MIT.

He has authored numerous books and articles including *On Becoming a Leader, Why Leaders Can't Lead, Managing People is Like Herding Cats: Bennis on Leadership, Leaders, An Invented Life: Reflections on Leadership and Change, Geeks and Geezers: How Era, Values and Deciding Moments Shape Leaders.*

He is a consultant to many Fortune 500 companies.

Guru's contribution

Warren Bennis has been described as guru of all gurus as far as leadership is concerned. In his book *On Becoming a Leader*[30] he presents the following basics of leadership:

- Leadership is a guiding vision.

- Leadership is a passion.

- Leadership is integrity which involves self-knowledge, candour and maturity.

- Leadership is curiosity.

- Leadership is daring.

In distinguishing leaders from managers, he wrote, *"I tend to think of the differences between leaders and managers as the differences between those who master the context and those who surrender to it. There are other differences as well, and they are enormous and crucial.*

- *The manager administers; the leader innovates.*

- *The manager is a copy; the leader is an original.*

- *The manager maintains; the leader develops.*

- *The manager focuses on systems and structure; the leader focuses on people.*

- *The manager relies on control; the leader inspires trust.*

- *The manager has a short-range view; the leader has a long-range perspective.*

- *The manager asks how and when; the leader asks what and why.*

---

30 Bennis, Warren (1989). '*On Becoming a Leader*'. Hutchison.

- *The manager has his eyes always on the bottom-line; the leader has his eye on the horizon.*

- *The manager imitates; the leader originates.*

- *The manager accepts the status quo; the leader challenges it.*

- *The manager is the classic good soldier; the leader is his own person.*

- *The manager does things right; the leader does the right thing."*

In his interview[31] Bennis said, *"Today's organisations are evolving into federations, networks, clusters, cross-functional teams, temporary systems, ad hoc task forces, lattices, modules, matrices – almost anything but pyramids with their obsolete top-down leadership. The new leader will encourage healthy dissent and values those followers courageous enough to say so.*

This does not mark the end of leadership – but rather the need for a new, far more subtle and indirect form of influence for leaders to be effective. The new reality is that intellectual capital (brain power, knowledge and human imagination) has supplanted capital as the critical success factor; leaders will have to learn an entirely new set of skills that are not understood nor taught in our business schools and, for all of those reasons, rarely practiced."

Bennis also commented that, *"the future has no shelf life. Future leaders will need a passion for continual learning, a refined, discerning ear for the moral and ethical consequences of their actions, and an understanding of the purpose of work and human organisations."*

---

31 Brown, Crainer, Dearlove and Rodrigues (2002). *'Business Minds'*, Financial Times/Prentice Hall.

He outlined four competencies that will determine the success of new leadership. They are:

1 The new leader understands and practises the power of appreciation.

2 The new leader keeps reminding people of what is important.

3 The new leader sustains and generates trust.

4 The new leader and the led are intimate allies.

In his article The Leadership advantage[32], he cites the following qualities of a leader:

*"**Technical competence**: business literacy and grasp of one's field.*

***Conceptual skill**: a facility for abstract or strategic thinking.*

***Track record**: a history of achieving results.*

***People skills**: an ability to communicate, motivate and delegate.*

***Taste**: an ability to identify and cultivate talent.*

***Judgement**: making difficult decisions in a short timeframe with imperfect data.*

***Character**: the qualities that define who you are.*

Senior executives seldom lack the first three attributes; rarely do they fail because of technical or conceptual incompetence, nor do they reach high levels of responsibility without having a strong track record. All these skills are important, but in tomorrow's world exemplary leaders will be distinguished by their mastery of the softer side: people skills, taste, judgement, and above all, character.

---

32 'The Leadership Advantage' by Warren Bennis. Leader to Leader, No. 12 Spring 1999. http://www.leadertoleader.org.

Exemplary leaders believe they have a responsibility to extend people's growth and to create an environment where people constantly learn. Those are the surest ways to generate intellectual capital and to use that capital to create new value. In the next century, that will be every leader's ultimate task."

Geeks and geezers

Warren Bennis with Robert J. Thomas published a book entitled *Geeks and Geezers: How Era, Values and Defining Moments Shape Leaders.*[33] The book looks at two categories of people – Geeks (come of age during 1991-2000) grew up 'virtual, visual and digital' and Geezers (come of age during 1945- 1954) shaped by World War II. Their research suggested that the core essentials of leadership remained constant across generations.

The basic premise of the book is that all leaders go through a 'crucible' of some kind. The different periods and environments affect the needs, characters and maturation processes of these people and, therefore, defines the differences in leadership style.

These are the following differences between Geeks and Geezers:

- Geeks are more ambitious than Geezers.

- Geeks place a greater value on balancing work–family life.

- Geeks are less likely to have heroes or leadership role models than Geezers.

This book promotes our understanding of the value and importance of 'crucibles' and in our understanding of training leaders who have gone through life-changing times.

---

33 Warren Bennis and Robert Thomas (2002). *'Geeks and Geezers: How Era, values and Defining Moments Shape Leaders'*, Harvard Business School Press.

Leadership crucibles are intense and shape a leader's self-understanding of his or her ability to adapt to a changing world. The study uncovered that self-development plays a critical role.

To understand what 'Geeks' appreciate also opens up different avenues of managing such 'Geeks'.

Lessons learnt from Warren Bennis

- A leader has to be innovative.

- A leader has responsibility for developing talent.

- A leader should institutionalise trust throughout the organisation.

- A leader has to work as partners with today's knowledge workers.

- A leader has to create a thriving work environment.

- A leader has to understand the needs of his followers.

- A leader appreciates and facilitates the realisation of the full potential of intellectual capital.

- In tomorrow's world exemplary leaders will be distinguished by their mastery of the softer side: people skills, taste, judgement, and, above all, character.

- Leadership is not solely the preserve of those at the top of the organisation.

- Trust is 'the emotional glue that binds followers and leaders together'.

- The two sources of leadership are individual and organisation setting.

- Learning to be an effective leader is no different than learning to be an effective person.

ELEVEN
Rosabeth Moss Kanter (1943-)

"The twentieth century was the age of machine;
the twenty-first century will be the age of people."

ROSABETH MOSS KANTER

Guru's profile

Rosabeth Moss Kanter who was born in 1943 is Ernest L. Arbuckle Professor of Business Administration at Harvard Business School. She joined the Harvard Business School faculty in 1986 from Yale University. She has received numerous honorary doctorates and about a dozen leadership awards. She has been named top of the list of the '50 most influential business thinkers in the world', one of the top 20 business gurus and 50th most powerful women in the world. She advises major corporations and various governments.

Guru's contribution

Professor Kanter specialises in strategy, innovation and leadership. For the purpose of this book I have singled out Professor Kanter's contribution in relation to managing people.

Empowerment

organisations should make power more accessible. Empowering your employees facilitates innovation.

"An innovating organisation needs a workforce at all levels that have not become stuck in the rhythm of routine jobs that it cannot easily adapt to a new drumbeat. For change to be a way of life rather than an occasional traumatising shock, the 'Indians' as well as the 'Chiefs' have to be engaged in change making and change mastery – while still doing their necessary jobs." [34]

Innovative organisations should involve their employees in coming up with innovative ideas. organisational culture should get rid of the segmentation of the organisation – only middle or top level people get involved in innovation.

Employees who are empowered and are involved in innovation become more satisfied with their jobs and therefore more productive. Managing people in an innovative organisation is about giving the opportunity to people to develop and to make a contribution to strategic objectives.

"Employees can be energised – engaged in problem solving and mobilised for change – by their involvement in a participative structure that permits them to venture beyond their normal work roles to tackle meaningful issues. They gain an experience of the communitas of teamwork on a special project – to use Victor Turner's term for dramas of high involvement – which lifts them out of the humdrum, repetitive routines of their place in the ongoing structure." [35]

Writing about post-industrial organisations, Kanter says, *"Post-entrepreneurial strategies hold out the promise of more satisfaction and rewards for people, but more of those benefits are contingent on what the individual – and the team – does and not on what the corpo-*

---

34 Rosabeth Moss Kanter (1983). *'The Change Masters'* Unwin Paperbacks. Pp181

35 ibid pp 203.

ration automatically provides. ...the excitement of projects in which people are empowered to act on their own ideas make work more satisfying and more absorbing, increasing the sense of accomplishment. The opportunity to be essentially in business for oneself, inside or outside the large corporation, puts more control in the hands of smaller groups. And because these consequences of the shift to post-entrepreneurial strategies are more motivating for people, the corporation should reap benefits, too, in increased productivity."[36]

Motivating your staff

Rosabeth Moss Kanter suggests the following guidelines for praising excellent performance and celebrating achievements:

PRINCIPLE 1

Emphasise success rather than failure. You tend to miss the positives if you are busily searching for the negatives.

PRINCIPLE 2

Deliver recognition and reward in an open and publicised way. If not made public, recognition loses much of its impact and defeats much of the purpose for which it is provided.

PRINCIPLE 3

Deliver recognition in a personal and honest manner. Avoid providing recognition that is too 'slick' or overproduced.

PRINCIPLE 4

Tailor your recognition and reward to the unique needs of the people involved. Having many recognition and reward options will enable

---

36 Rosabeth Moss Kanter (1989). 'When Giants Learn to Dance', Simon & Schuster. Pp 356.

managers to acknowledge accomplishment in ways appropriate to the particulars of a given situation, selecting from a large menu of possibilities.

PRINCIPLE 5

Timing is crucial. *recognise* contribution throughout a project. Reward contribution close to the time an achievement is realised. Time delays weaken the impact of most rewards.

PRINCIPLE 6

Strive for a clear, unambiguous and well-communicated connection between accomplishments and rewards. Be sure people understand why they receive awards and the criteria used to determine rewards.

PRINCIPLE 7

recognise recognition. That is, recognise people who recognise others for doing what is best for the company.[37]

Leadership

organisations have been subjected to three external forces, namely, Globalisation, information technology and industry consolidation. In a changing business climate, the role of a leader in change adept organisations is to:

- encourage innovation;

- deliver personal competence;

- to be open and honest;

- extend the organisation reach;

---

37 Rosabeth Moss Kanter – '*Holiday Gift – Celebrating Employee Achievements*', Management Review, December 1986.

- to be proactive to discontinuity; and

- to listen to customers.

Leaders, besides possessing passion, conviction and confidence, should work with his/her followers as partners in change. He/she should create a network of listening posts.

They also have to create 'kaleidoscope thinking' – fit different parts of the organisation together. Constantly review assumptions about your business. Look to shake up the pattern of your business. It is also important to communicate your aspiration. Form a coalition with your employees and partners. Provide support by way of resources and coaching. Be involved in the change process. One of the mistakes leaders make in a change process is to launch them and leave them. recognise, reward and celebrate achievements.[38]

Professor Kanter was asked, 'What style of leadership do you like today?'

"I must say that today I see many of the same characteristics that I was talking about – a free and open spirit of inquiry. Willingness to challenge orthodoxy and assumptions, and to chart new direction.

My definition of leadership is that which leaves the world a better and different place, that is you lead people in a new direction to solve problems and make new things happen. You stretch people to achieve things they didn't think were possible. So it starts with that same spirit of dialogue and curiosity and of leaders seeing that there is still work to be done; that is we haven't solved every problem, we have not improved the world sufficiently. They then challenge assumptions, chart new directions and inspire others with the power of their vision. They create a support system or structure that makes it possible to get the resources and credibility. They nurture a team that does the actual work, they persist, and they make heroes out of all the people who have worked with them."[39]

---

38 These points have been extracted from 'The Enduring Skills of Change Leaders' by Rosabeth Moss Kanter. Leader to Leader No. 13, Summer, 1999.

39 Interview with Ivy Business Journal.

Lessons learnt from Rosabeth Moss Kanter

- Leaders should have conviction, commitment and be effective communicators.

- They should be good listeners.

- They should question business assumptions constantly.

- They should be passionate and form coalitions.

- They should transmit values and priorities to all the employees in the organisation.

- They should facilitate learning in the organisation.

- Leaders in a modern world have to be focused, fast, flexible, friendly and fair.

- Disregard the 'boss' mentality and adopt the 'partner' mentality.

TWELVE
Peter Senge (1947-)

"A learning organisation is a group of people who are continually enhancing their capabilities to create what they want to create."

PETER SENGE

Guru's profile

Peter Senge was born in 1947 He is a senior lecturer at the Massachusetts Institute of Technology. He received a B.S. in Engineering from Stanford University and an M.S. in Social Systems Modelling and a Ph.D. in Management from MIT.

His areas of special interest focus on decentralising the role of leadership in organisations in order to enhance the capacity of employees to work effectively.

His book *The Fifth Discipline: The art and Practice of the Learning organisation* (1990) became widely acclaimed. Harvard Business Review identified his book as one of the seminal management books of the past 57 years.

Guru's contribution

Dr. Senge established his name in the field of Learning organisation. He has enabled many leading edge corporations to improve their learning capacity.

The learning organisation

According to Peter Senge, there are five essential disciplines for a learning organisation:

1 Personal mastery.

2 Mental models.

3 Shared vision.

4 Team learning.

5 Systems thinking.

These disciplines relate to " *a shift of mind from seeing parts to seeing wholes, from seeing people as helpless reactors to seeing them as active participants in shaping their reality, from reacting to the present to creating the future.* "[40]

Learning organisations are *"organisations where people continually expand their capacity to create the results they truly desire, where new and expansive patterns of thinking are nurtured, where collective aspiration is set free, and where people are continually learning to see the whole together."* [41]

---

40 Ibid. pp 69

41 Peter M. Senge (1990). 'The Fifth Discipline: The Art & Practice of the Learning organisation'. Century. Pp.3

The emphasis is on people within organisations wanting to learn and wanting to develop their talent facilitated by organisational culture. Managing people within the context of the learning organisation demands a collaborative and tolerant culture that brings about alignment of organisational and personal goals. It is a culture that enables people to re-create themselves.

Personal mastery

Personal mastery is focused on individuals. It is individuals in the organisation who learn, create knowledge and transform knowledge into organisational knowledge.

Without individuals there is no learning. *"Personal mastery goes beyond competence and skills, though it is grounded in competence and skills. It goes beyond spiritual unfolding or opening, although it requires spiritual growth. It means approaching one's life as a creative work, living life from a creative as opposed to reactive viewpoint."* [42]

Components of personal mastery include individuals' values, continuously asking and clarifying what is important and learning to see reality more clearly. This discipline is very difficult to understand for hard-nosed business people. Nevertheless, personal mastery is very important for workers who have different values and aspirations and want an opportunity to examine themselves. Personal mastery is about total self-development.

Mental models

Each individual has an 'internal' image of the world based on certain assumptions. Individual behaviour is guided by these mental models which are the result of our experience, education and environment.

---

42 ibid. pp141.

Mental models can and do, constitute barriers to learning. If we perceive that the organisation we work for does not care for our development or aspirations, or is unfair in its dealings, we will act accordingly by not making an effective contribution to the organisation. (The 'I am not all right- you are not all right' syndrome.)

Mental models affect us in a way we make decisions and behave interpersonally. *"The discipline of mental models starts with turning the mirror inward; learning to unearth our internal pictures of the world, to bring them to the surface and hold them rigorously to scrutiny."* [43]

Shared vision

Shared vision incorporates the involvement of many individuals. Everyone in the organisation has to understand the vision of the business and be involved in implementing it. A shared vision gives meaning to work and it prompts contribution and effort. It is an effective incentive for learning – a way of winning the 'hearts and minds' of employees.

When vision is shared the task becomes part of the self. *"When there is a genuine vision (as opposed to the all-to-familiar 'vision statement'), people excel and learn, not because they are told to, but because they want to."* [44]

Team learning

Individuals brainstorm, have conversations, exchange experiences, work on projects in teams. People need to be able to work together.

At the end of each project or assignment, team members can reflect on achievements, their competencies and their experiences. Team learning generates synergy within the organisation.

---

43 Ibid. pp 9.

44 ibid pp9.

Systems thinking

The Fifth Discipline.

Systems thinking integrates the other four disciplines and it enables the organisation to see the 'big picture'. Systems thinking is fundamental to any learning organisation. Without systems thinking, each of the other disciplines will be isolated, which will not help generate organisational learning.

Criticisms of Peter Senge's theory

- It is too philosophical and sophisticated for practising managers.

- organisations are interested in short-term results.

- Employees in western cultures are not used to turning their mirrors inward.

- organisations define learning in a narrow way – learning to them is about training their employees to be efficient.

- It ignores the existence of organisational politics.

- organisations in general are interested in quick fixes to satisfy their key stakeholders.

Lessons learnt from Peter Senge

- We learn best from our experience.

- Not appreciating the importance of systems theory leads to a culture of blame and defensive behaviour.

- Individual learning leads to organisational learning.

- A culture of learning facilitates development of talent and new orientations.

- Share corporate vision throughout your organisation.

- Learning organisations motivate individuals to work in teams effectively and to promote honest and open communication.

- Learning organisations require a new view of leadership.

- Learning organisations demand leaders who are inspirational and who can act as designers, stewards and teachers.

- Leaders should be responsible for creating an environment which is conducive to people developing new capabilities.

- Do not confuse rank with leadership.

THIRTEEN
Geert Hofstede (1928-)

"Every person carries within him or herself patterns of thinking, feeling and potential acting which were learned throughout their lifetime."

GEERT HOFSTEDE

Guru's profile

Geert Hofstede was born in 1928. He received his M.Sc. from Deft Institute of Technology in 1953 and his Ph.D. from Groningen University in 1967. His career has moved between industry and academia.

Guru's contribution

Dr. Hofstede became well-known for his work in cultural studies. He presented four dimensions of culture. They are power Distance, Individualism and Collectivism, Masculinity and Femininity, and Uncertainty Avoidance. Hofstede describes culture as the *"collective programming of the mind"*.

Power distance: He defines Power Distance as *"the extent to which the less powerful members of institutions and organisations within a country express and accept that power is distributed equally."*[45]

---

45 Geert Hofsted (1994). 'Cultures and organisations: Software of the Mind', HarperCollins. Pp28

People in a high power distance culture are comfortable with the status accorded to various groups of people. In terms of leadership they have a high dependence on their bosses. Their preferences are for an autocratic type of leadership.

"Popular management literature on 'leadership' often forgets that leadership can only exist as a complement to 'subordinateship'. The moral for managers is: if you want to know how your subordinates see you, don't try to look in the mirror; that just produces wishful thinking. Turn around 180 degrees and face your own boss."

organisations in a high power distance culture centralise power. The structure is very hierarchical. Superiors are entitled to privileges.

In a low power distance culture equality prevails and the situation is opposite to high power distance situations.

Individualism and collectivism

Such a culture emphasises the degree the society reinforces individual or collective achievement. Individuals under an individual's culture are supposed to look after him or her, and personal relationships are loose. In collectivism interpersonal relationships are strong and group needs rank higher than those of individuals.

Individuals prefer to have time on their hands and freedom to pursue challenges. organisations employing such people should structure jobs or tasks to meet such needs.

In a collectivist culture it is important for individuals to work within groups and teams and group loyalty becomes important.

organisation cultures differ depending on individualist or collectivist culture. This has implications for managing people depending on whether you are managing within an individualist culture, in which case performance is monitored on an individual basis, or a collectivist culture, in which case performance is based on team or group work.

Masculinity and femininity

A high masculine culture focuses on the high degree the society rein-forces the work role model of male achievement. Such role emphasises the importance of earning, recognition, advancement and challenge. *"In a masculine society, the ethos tends more toward 'live in order to work'.*[46]

A high femininity culture emphasises the importance of good working relationships, co-operation and security. Conflict is resolved by negotiation and compromise.

The leadership style in a masculine culture is more geared towards being assertive and decisive, and making decisions without consul-tation. In a feminine culture, on the other hand, a leader likes to arrive at a decision by consensus.

Uncertainty avoidance

This reflects the level of tolerance for uncertainty and ambiguity within the society. A high uncertainty avoidance shows a low tolerance for uncertainty and vice versa. In such a situation laws and rules prevail in abundance.

"In terms of leadership and innovation, weak uncertainty avoidance leads to tolerance of mistakes and encouragement to be innovative. According to Hofstede, differences in uncertainty avoidance imply differ-ences in motivation patterns but the picture becomes clearer when we simultaneously consider the masculinity-femininity dimension."[47]

---

46 ibid pp93.

47 Ibid pp123.

Criticisms of Hofstede's theory

- The theory is much generalised and is based on faulty assumptions.

- His questionnaires were culturally biased.

- He ignored the existence of plurality of cultures within an organisation.

Despite these criticisms Hofstede's theory has become very popular as far as understanding of national cultures is concerned and their implications within the context of doing business across borders.

Lessons learnt from Geert Hofstede

- People behave differently in different cultures.

- An insight into different cultures promotes our understanding of how to manage people effectively.

- Cultural studies enhance the performance of multi-cultural teams.

- Cultural studies minimise misunderstanding and improves collaboration between businesses across various cultures.

- Leaders must recognise the importance and influence of differing cultures.

- Culture differences should influence the organisation mission and value statements.

FOURTEEN
Ikujiro Nonaka (1935-)

"Innovation process is not simply information processing. It's a process to capture create, leverage and retain knowledge."

IKUJIRO NONAKA

Guru's profile

Professor Ikukiro Nonaka was born in 1935 and obtained his degree in Politics and Economics at Waseda University. He gained his Doctorate from Berkeley College of California State University in 1972.

Guru's contribution

Nonaka made his name in the field of knowledge management. All organisations, big or small, for profit and not-for-profit, have to make decisions within the context of changes taking place inside the organisation and in the external environment.

Changes in the socio-economic environment, changes in market conditions, changes in political ideologies and so on, all affect how we do our business today. It is imperative for long-term survival to monitor these changes and collect information. Collecting information and building all kinds of database is not enough. This information has to be put into context and used. This practice leads to the creation and use of knowledge.

Knowledge is an appreciating asset; the more it is used the more effective its application. There is a big difference in data, information and knowledge. organisational knowledge is not about IT. The following article presents a down-to-earth explanation of the nature of knowledge and its importance.

Managing knowledge without tears
– by Sultan Kermally

> "...the truly revolutionary impact of the Information Revolution is not artificial intelligence, information, or the effect of computers and data processing on decision-making, policy making or strategy. The key to continued growth and Leadership in the New Economy is not electronics of computers but the cognitive skills of the 'knowledge workers'."
>
> PETER DRUCKER

Before exploring the importance of managing knowledge and Knowledge workers it is important to dispel the following myths about managing knowledge:

MYTH NO 1
KNOWLEDGE MANAGEMENT IS ABOUT TECHNOLOGY.
Wrong. Knowledge as such has nothing to do with technology.

Technology is merely an enabler. Knowledge is about PEOPLE and how they are managed to collaborate and share their experiences and trust one another in exchanging knowledge gained.

MYTH NO. 2
MANAGING KNOWLEDGE REQUIRES THE APPOINTMENT OF KNOWL-EDGE SPECIALISTS AND THE ACQUISITION OF KNOWLEDGE SYSTEMS

Wrong. Employees are 'knowledge workers' and what is needed is not the appointment of specialists but enthusiasts or knowledge champions. One does not require purchasing specialists systems to spending an additional dollar on computers or so-called knowledge management systems.

MYTH NO. 3
KNOWLEDGE MANAGEMENT IS A FAD AND SOMETHING VERY NEW ADVOCATED BY CONSULTANTS

Wrong. Knowledge management is not a fad; it is here to stay. It is also not new, or it is as new as Egyptian pyramids. Some countries and organisations have been managing knowledge for a number of years, for example 3M and Scandia. 3M since they have started doing business have managed to sustain innovation by encouraging employees to share their knowledge and Scandia, as a result of their experience in managing knowledge, have highlighted the importance of human capital in assessing the performance of their organisation. It has become imperative now for all organisations including SMEs because of Globalisation and internetisation of businesses and markets. We now do business in market space as opposed to market place.

Why has managing knowledge become important for all organisations now?

organisations now face the following challenges:

- Increasing value of the intellectual capital is embedded in end products and services.

- There has been an increasing convergence of technologies that is enabling organisations to globalise at the press of the button.

- There is a rapid growth of Internet.

> In summary, Economies are increasingly based on knowledge. What's new is that a growing chunk of production in the modern economy is in the form of intangibles, based on the exploitation of ideas rather than material things.
>
> *Economist Newspaper.* September, 23, 2000.

Many organisations are resisting the adopting of knowledge management because most of them have gone through the traumas of reengineering, de-layering and restructuring. Some of the employees have gone through very bad times over the past two decades. They do not want or are not ready to jump through yet another hoop.

However, the way business is structured nowadays and with the advent of the New Economy (which is here to stay in spite of the bombing of dot-coms) managing knowledge has become business imperative if the organisations have to gain and sustain competitive advantage. Given that, it is imperative what is meant by managing knowledge. There are as many definitions of knowledge management as there are experts in this area. In basic terms, managing knowledge is about creating an environment where people within the organisation trust one another and trust leadership to share and create knowledge so that organisations can win new business and compete efficiently. Creating such an environment involves changing the culture of the organisation and putting processes in place to enable knowledge creation and transfer.

Differences between data, information and knowledge

Data is unorganised words, numbers and images. It has no meaning or context. The name Sultan Kermally in a database is merely data. The statement 'Sultan Kermally is a regular customer of our products' is information. Information is organised or categorised data.

Knowledge is the use of information. An organisation using the information that 'Sultan Kermally is a regular customer of our products' take initiatives to establish a special relationship with the customer, thus creating customer knowledge. If the information gained is not used then the knowledge remains passive. It cannot be considered as an active intangible asset. Similarly, if employees have skills but they do not use them then such skills remain passive and of no benefit to the organisation. organisations can, therefore, gather/capture information about their customers, their employees, their competitors and so on. They can become knowledge-driven organisations if they have the culture and processes to use the information. This is what knowledge management is all about.

Information and experiences of specific individuals are tacit knowledge. If the organisation puts processes in place to make this knowledge explicit so that other employees acquire this knowledge and USE it, then that organisation is facilitating knowledge creation and transfer. The initiatives that can be put in place include coaching, shadowing, training workshops, after-action reviews, building skills directory and so on. The focus of attention in designing and introducing any initiative is to ask, 'Does that initiative promote knowledge sharing – does it facilitate transformation of knowledge from being tacit or implicit to being explicit?'

Knowledge is the source of innovation. The application of knowledge enhances the capability of the organisation and the outcome brings about innovation.

Making a start – some examples/initiatives

Begin to build an experience directory. If, for example, you are a Project Management Company then ask each of your employees to answer some key questions, say about ten questions after they have experienced completion of a project. The questions should draw out the nature of the project, the challenges involved and the way these challenges were attended to, and the person/persons involved in the project. The result will be the creation of an experience directory. The information should be made available to all project leaders. Such an initiative will stop reinventing a wheel, save cost and encourage exchange of information and creation of organisational knowledge.

The other initiative would be to capture information on what employees currently do, what they could do, given the opportunity, and what they would like to do (their aspirations) if they could acquire new skills.

The organisation can transform this information in formulating stretch objectives for their employees and for preparing developmental objectives that could be used for new business development.

Knowledge is also power – why should employees share this power?

Knowledge is an appreciating asset. The more it is shared the more it is enhanced. If an organisation has effective leadership and if the culture of the organisation is conducive to people trusting one another, then employees or 'knowledge-workers' will be glad to 'empower' their colleagues by sharing their knowledge.

At the end of the day, whether the organisation becomes knowledge-driven depends on leadership, culture and trust. There are many examples in practice of some organisations and teams creating initiatives to share and create knowledge without individual or organisational tears. Such organisations include Sun Microsystems, Microsoft, Chevron, Xerox, Bankers Trust and Shell.

Employees have come together to create knowledge for their organisations.

According to a Brazilian proverb, 'When we dream alone it is a dream. When we dream together, it is the beginning of reality'.

What is an incentive for your organisation to manage knowledge?

Think about a big chunk of your intangible asset in a form of human capital walking out of the door every evening. This is your most valuable asset which you have to nurture and motivate.

Final thought

Remember...

> *"organisations are perfectly designed for the result they achieve."*
>
> PAUL GUSTAVSON

Please note: In this article several statements are made about some companies taking initiatives to motivate their staff to share and transfer knowledge. In my book *New Economy Energy: Unleashing Knowledge for Competitive Advantage* (2001) published by John Wiley, I provide case studies of the following companies who have taken several initiatives to become knowledge-driven organisations:

- Microsoft
- ICL
- Becton Dickson

- Apple Japan

- Chevron

- Sun Microsystems

Professor Nonaka and managing knowledge

Professor Nonaka together with his colleague Hiro Takeuchi put knowledge in the forefront of the business agenda. Creation, sharing and use of knowledge depends on how people in the organisation are managed.[48]

They have presented the SECI model – socialisation, externalisation, combination and internalisation processes generate, transfer and transform knowledge within the organisation.

Most of the knowledge in an organisation is in the form of tacit knowledge – knowledge in peoples' heads. This tacit knowledge is personal, context-specific and hard to communicate. However, it is important to transform this tacit knowledge as far as it is possible, into explicit knowledge in order to share it organisationally. **To do so will depend on how you manage people**.

The interaction between tacit knowledge and explicit knowledge brings about the following four modes of knowledge conversion:

- socialisation.

- externalisation.

- Combination.

- internalisation.

---

48 Ikujiro Nonaka and Hirotaka Takeuchi (1995). '*The knowledge-Creating Company: How Japanese Companies Create the Dynamics of Innovation.*' Oxford.

socialisation

It is a way of capturing an individual's tacit knowledge. It occurs by sharing experiences and on-the-job learning. These experiences are shared openly and the individuals have to be motivated to be involved in the socialisation process. The knowledge conversion is from individual tacit to group tacit.

externalisation

This is the process of converting group tacit knowledge into explicit knowledge. At this stage tacit knowledge is converted into models, prototypes and hypotheses. This knowledge can be used to come up with new products or processes

Combination

This mode transforms explicit knowledge into further explicit knowledge by embedding knowledge into documents, manuals and so on.

internalisation

This is the process of transforming explicit knowledge into tacit knowledge. Individuals internalise their experiences in performing specific functions or tasks. This mode is all about 'learning-by-doing'.

organisations have to put processes in place in order to become knowledge-based. However, for individuals the fundamental question, 'What's in it for me?' have to be addressed in order to make processes effective. The way the question is answered depends on organisational culture, leadership and the type of motivation presented.

Managing knowledge is about creating a collaborative culture that will facilitate open communication and institutionalise trust. It is about managing people in the knowledge era.

Criticisms of the SECI model

- The model is cultural-biased.

- It is based on the experience of Japanese companies which do business in different type of structures to those in Western culture.

- Some have argued it is not knowledge as such but the act of knowing and use of knowledge that enables organisations to capture and sustain competitive advantage.

Lessons learnt from Professor Nonaka

- Individuals are your most important asset.

- The raison d'etre of a firm is to continuously create knowledge.

- Knowledge is an important strategic asset.

- Most knowledge is tacit knowledge located in peoples' heads.

- organisations have to create a collaborative environment in order to facilitate knowledge creation and transfer.

- Effective leaders have to address the 'What's in it for me?' question to their workers.

- Managing knowledge at the end of the day, is about managing people.

FIFTEEN
Charles Handy (1932-)

"We must not let our past, however glorious;
get in the way of our future."

CHARLES HANDY

Guru's profile

Charles Handy was born in Ireland in 1932. He is a graduate of Oxford University gaining degree in Classics, History and Philosophy. He worked for Shell International for a few years and subsequently went to Sloan School of Management at MIT. After obtaining his MBA he returned to England.

He was appointed Professor at the London Business School in 1972. In 1987 he was commissioned to undertake a comparative study of management development in America, Japan, Britain and Europe.

He is a writer and broadcaster, and consultant to a wide variety of organisations, government, for profit and not-for-profit organisations.

Guru's contribution

In this his first book, *Understanding organisations* (1976), Professor Handy presented his motivation calculus which pulled together the various strands of different motivational theories.

There are three components to his motivation model – needs, results and effectiveness (the E factor).

Needs

Needs as categorised by Maslow (see chapter four on Abraham Maslow). Needs as explained by Herzberg (see chapter six on Frederick Herzberg). These needs are relative, dynamic and change over time.

Results

We should measure the effect of the outcomes achieved.

Effectiveness

Have the results met our needs? The feedback that the model provides.

Each calculus operates within the limit of a psychological contract. This type of contract is an implied contract between employee and an employer. An individual expects his personal objectives to be fulfilled by joining an organisation and the organisation expects an individual to achieve the organisational objectives set. Individuals will be motivated when the psychological contract, as viewed by the organisation and by the individual, becomes the same.

"That there is no 'right' theory of motivation, but only the individual and the particular circumstances."

What are the implications of this model in practice?

"Managers need to think more deeply and more clearly about their view of the psychological contract operating in their organisation.

Moral: The psychological contract will be a significant factor in the choice of leadership style and the organisation of work.

If managers wish to change the method of control or the method of influence in their organisation they must be aware that they are changing the psychological contract.

Moral: the psychological contract often lies at the heart of any change problem.

If the desired outcome of a decision reached by means of the motivation calculus is not working out, i.e. if the individual finds that his expectancy calculation is wrong and ' E' does not lead to the expected results, he experiences 'dissonance'." [49]

Dissonance leads to stress at work and it needs to be resolved by increasing the 'E' factor in motivation calculus.

Leadership

Handy believes that various leadership theories such as trait theories, style theories and contingency theories all have something to offer in examining what makes leadership effective. However, effective leadership depends on the leader (his preferred style, his values, his confidence, his contribution), the subordinates (their preferred style of leadership in a given situation, their psychological contract, their experience, their culture), the task (the complexity, the timescale involved, the importance) and the environment (organisational culture, the structure and the technology of the organisation, the nature of the followers, the power position of the leader).

The effectiveness of a leader will be materialised if the leader, the subordinates and the task fit together. Such fit will depend on the environment, the organisational setting, and the leader. The individual's leader ability to adapt becomes an important factor.

---

49 Charles Handy (1976). 'Understanding organisations' Penguin Books. Pp 38-48.

In addition, a leader has to assume an ambassadorial role and also act as a model.

organisational culture

Professor Handy puts forward the view that cultures of organisations differ. These cultures are reflected in organisational structures and systems. He classifies organisational cultures into (a) the power culture, (b) the role culture, (c) the task culture, and (d) the person culture.

The power culture is represented by small enterprises. Power in this type of organisation is centralised. In this type of organisation there are few rules and procedures and very little bureaucracy.

The role culture is often represented by bureaucratic structure. There are rules and procedures and these are coordinated by senior management. The focus in this type of organisation is on the role, rather than individuals or groups.

The task culture is project oriented. The focus is on getting the job done. Individuals are experts and the culture is adapted depending on the nature of the projects. This type of culture is good at responding to market needs.

The person culture. In this type of culture the focus is on individuals and their professionalism.

It is important to analyse and appreciate different organisational cultures as psychological contracts differ according to differing cultures. To manage individuals effectively there has to be an alignment between the individual contract and the organisational contract.

'Our employees are our greatest asset'

Employees should be considered as assets rather than a cost. Many organisations do not hold this view though they do institute systems and procedures to bring about appraisal systems, career planning and compensation systems for their employees.

In managing people it is important to consider dominant cultures within organisations. Different cultures will determine how people are managed in different organisations. Cultures also determine the way individuals develop their talent.[50]

Inside organisations [51]

In this book Professor Handy reinforces the importance of satisfying human needs and enhancing the 'E' factor and also the nature of the psychological contract.

He also introduces the concept or the theory of 'The Inside-out Doughnut'. The things which you must do are spelt out for you but filling the empty space in your doughnut is left to your discretion and initiative.

As organisations get flatter the empty space of the doughnut becomes larger and the type of talent needed to fill the space changes. *"Managing people with large do'nuts can be worrying – you cannot know what they are doing all the time. As with the enterprising child, you want to encourage them to be independent, but what if they get it wrong? To manage their do'nuts you must specify the core with great care, then at least you know that the essential tasks will be understood and the key rules kept; the outside boundaries of the do'nut must also be well understood: Do not go outside here."*[52]

---

50 Interesting account of the methods used to develop talent within different cultural context is given in 'understanding organisations'. Pp262-295.

51 Charles Handy (1990) 'Inside organisations': 21 Ideas for Managers. BBC Books.

52 Ibid. Pp60.

He also makes the point that in a modern business climate companies have increasingly taken on a shamrock shape. The shamrock is represented by three leaves which he labels as the core workforce, the contractual fringe and the flexible workforce.

The core workforce gives their organisation its uniqueness. Because they are the core workforce the organisation makes an effort to retain them.

The contractual fringe represents the workforce outside the organisation. These are independent contractors, outsourced workers and so on.

Finally, there is the flexible labour force which is the organisation casual labour force and part-timers, or people working on a flexi hour's basis. *"The way things are going it may well be that there will be more people working outside the core than inside it by the end of the century."*[53]

He also says that *"most people working today will become portfolio people for some part of their working lives, like it or not."*[54]

Implications for managing people

The shamrock organisation, the do'nut theory and portfolio workers, all present daunting challenges for today's leaders. The style and the nature of leadership have to change in order to manage people effectively. One has to take into account the nature of business, the structure of the organisation, the organisational culture and the types of workforce in order to motivate and lead effectively.

Professor Handy also published books entitled *The Age of Unreason, Beyond Certainty, The Empty Raincoat* and *The Hungary Spirit* in which he emphasises the changing structure of business and the changing

---

53 Ibid. Pp 206

54 Ibid. Pp 217.

nature of the workforce, the age of uncertainty and planning for the future. These changes have a direct impact on the way we manage people.

Lessons learnt from Charles Handy

- Individuals have needs and they work to get these needs fulfilled.

- It is important to align an individual's aspirations with the organisational aspirations.

- organisations should consider seriously the existence of the psychological contract at the time of recruitment.

- Psychological contracts differ with differing organisational structure.

- To manage people effectively consider the nature of environment, the tasks involved and organisational objectives.

- The business world is becoming increasing uncertain. To manage uncertainty and complexity develop the talent of individuals in order to achieve 'strategic fit'.

SIXTEEN

Peter Drucker (1909-)

"The flute part is an essential part of a Beethoven symphony. But by itself it is not music. It becomes music by being part of the 'score' that is by becoming an input which joins together with the inputs of sixty-five other musicians and their instruments."

PETER DRUCKER

Guru's profile

Peter Drucker is the father of management gurus; he is the guru of all gurus. When he speaks most CEOs pay attention. He was born in Vienna in 1909 and trained in Economics. He has subsequently become the world's foremost pioneer of management theory.

He is a teacher, consultant, writer and a speaker and has become the leading management gurus of his time. His first book, Concept of the Corporation (1946), was a groundbreaking examination of the internal workings of General Motors.

His management books The Practice of Management (1954), Management: Tasks Responsibilities, Practices (1973), Innovation and Entrepreneurship (1985), The Frontiers of Management (1986), and his recent books Peter Drucker on the Profession of Management (1998) and *Management Challenges for the 21st Century* (1999), have become international bestsellers.

He popularised concepts such as privatisation, management by objectives, decentralisation, knowledge worker and the knowledge economy – concepts which we now take for granted.

He is a Professor of Social Sciences and Management at the Claremont Graduate University, California which named its Graduate School of Management after him. In July 2002, President George Bush presented him with the Presidential Medal of Freedom, the Nation's highest civilian honour.

Guru's contribution

Peter Drucker's contribution is spread over most areas of management and business. Keeping to the theme of this book, I have extracted his various contributions in relation to 'managing people' from his various books:

People selection

"Executives spend more time on managing people and making people decisions than anything else, and they should. No other decisions are so long-lasting in their consequences or so difficult to unmake. And yet, by and large, executives make poor promotion and staffing decisions. In no other area of management would we put up with such miserable performance. Indeed we need not and should not." [55]

He gives guidelines as to what steps to take and what factors to consider in selecting staff. organisations simply do not think through what the job requirements are and whether a person can do the job or not.

---

55 Peter Drucker (1986) 'The Frontiers of Management', Butterworth-Heinemann. Pp119.

Self-development

Developing talent to meet personal, organisational and marketing needs has become one of the key features of managing people.

"Self-development of the effective executive is central to the development of the organisation, whether it is a business, a government agency, a research laboratory, a hospital or a military service. It is the way towards performance of the organisation. As executives work towards becoming effective, they raise the performance level of the whole organisation. They raise the sights of people – their own as well as others.

As a result, the organisation not only becomes capable of doing better. It becomes capable of doing different things and of aspiring to different goals. Developing executive effectiveness will challenge directions, goals, and purposes of organisation. It raises the egos of its people from preoccupation with problems to a vision of opportunity, from concern with weaknesses to exploitation of strengths. This, in turn, whenever it happens, makes an organisation attractive to people of high ability and aspiration and motivates people to higher performance and higher dedication. organisations are not more effective because they have better people. They have better people because they motivate to self-development, through their standards, through their habits, through their climate. And these, in turn, result from systematic, focused, purposeful self-training of the individuals in becoming effective executives." [56]

Manager development

In his book *The Practice of Management*, Drucker has a chapter on Developing Managers. He believes that management development is not about identifying talent for today's requirements but it should embrace developing managers to manage the future.

"But the men who need manager development the most are not the 'balls of fire' who are the back-up men and promo table people. They

---

56 Peter Drucker (1967) 'The Effective Executive', Heinemann Professional Publishing. Pp141.

are those managers who are not good enough to be promoted but not poor enough to be fired. These constitute the great majority; and they do the bulk of the actual management of the business. Most of them will, ten years hence, still be in their present jobs. Unless they have grown up to the demands of tomorrow's jobs, the whole management group will be inadequate – no matter how good, how carefully selected and developed, the promotable people. And whatever can be gained by developing the chosen few will be offset by the stunting, the malformation, and the resentment of those who are passed over." [57]

This is an extremely important point Drucker makes in terms of managing people in a modern business. There are many organisations including big consultancies, which have a system of identifying talent, by which they mean people who are or could be promotable to senior positions. They are given special training based on a so called 'fast-track' route. Such a practice in my opinion demotes the rest of the staff and creates a self-professing fulfilment based on the 'Pygmalion effect'. The message to the rest of the staff is 'you are presently tolerable but immediately dispensable'. Managing people under such a situation would be very difficult. *This is the culture of demotivation.*

Psychological contract

We have already introduced in an earlier chapter the concept and the importance of 'psychological contract'. Psychological contract is two-way traffic – reflecting organisational and individual demands. Apart from the legal contract of employment or a contract that delivers economic returns, there is also an implied contract on behalf of organisations and employees. Drucker does not use the name 'psychological contract' but in his chapter on Employing the Whole Man[58] he does mention that there are demands made by the enterprise on the worker and demands made by workers on the enterprise.

---

57 Peter Drucker (1967) 'The Practice of Management', Heinemann. Pp182.

58 Ibid. Pp261-264.

The demands made by the enterprise on the worker are:

- A fair day's work.

- Making efforts to achieve organisational objectives.

- Dedication.

- Taking responsibility.

- Willingness to accept change.

The worker's demands on the enterprise include:

- Fair day's pay.

- Fulfilment of status.

- Justice.

- Equal opportunities for advancement.

- Meaningful work.

This is what we understand, with some medications, is the nature of present day 'psychological contract'. Two sets of demands must be aligned for organisations to achieve their objects and for employees to meet their aspirations.

Motivation

In his chapter on Motivating to Peak Performance, Drucker points out the fact that job satisfaction on its own is adequate as motivation. He emphasises the importance of responsibility. Responsibility, according to Drucker, involves careful placement, high standards of performance, proper and adequate information and opportunities.

He advocates fixing stretch objectives so workers get self-motivated by the nature of the work itself.

Peter Senge emphasised the need for sharing vision for the organisation to become a learning organisation. Such an organisation creates a culture which motivates its employees. Drucker states, *"The worker will assume responsibility for peak performance only if he has managerial vision, that is, if he sees the enterprise as if he were a manager responsible, through his performance, for its success and survival. This vision he can only attain through the experience of participation."*[59]

In his book *Management: Tasks Responsibilities, Practices*[60], Drucker surveys some key motivational theories and comment on associated realities. He writes, in addition to accepting Theory Y (McGregor's theory) assumptions, *"Managers must further accept it as their job to make worker and working achieving. They must be willing, as a result, to accept high demands on themselves, their seriousness, and their competence. But managers cannot assume, as Theory Y does, that people will work to achieve if only they were given the opportunity to do so. More is needed – much more – to make even the strong and healthy accept the burden of responsibility."*[61]

Empowerment

We also talk about empowerment now and Rosabeth Moss Kanter (Chapter twelve) has stressed the importance of empowerment in today's business.

Empowerment is defined as an act of releasing human energy. It is about creating situations where workers share power and assume responsibility of making their decisions for the benefit of organisations and themselves.

To use a motivational perspective, it is about providing an opportunity to gain achievement, responsibility and advancement, and it is also about eliminating meaningless, powerlessness and isolation.

---

59 Ibid. Pp301.

60 Peter Drucker (1974) 'Management', Heinemann. pp220-232.

61 Ibid. Pp232.

Many senior managers are afraid to empower their staff. Some of the senior managers have worked a number of years gaining power, so giving it away or some of it away means less power for them.

Empowering people increases power – phenomenon of increasing returns. Empowering people goes hand in hand with creating opportunities for employees to make decisions.

Empowerment can be looked at from organisational as well as individual perspectives. organisations can create an appropriate and an enabling culture for empowerment to take place but at the end of the day it is individuals who have to empower themselves. They have to give commitment and involvement.

The whole chapter in Drucker's book on Motivating to Peak Performance is about empowering employees to achieve peak performance – only Drucker does not use the label 'empowerment'. He makes the point that modern management writers do, that you cannot give power to people – they have to accept power themselves. According to Drucker, pride and accomplishment cannot be given; it grows out of individuals.

He also has a lot to say about measuring performance. In his book *Practice of Management*[62], he makes the point that business needs objectives and it is employees who are asked to deliver these objectives. Once objectives are set then managers have to monitor them to see if they are attained. He advises managers to think through very carefully in managing meaningful measurement.

Leadership

Most of the leadership gurus emphasise the importance of substance rather than style in becoming an effective leader. Drucker in his book *Managing for the Future*[63] has a chapter on Leadership: More Doing

---

62 Peter Drucker (1955) 'Practice of Management', Heinemann. Pp147.

63 Peter Drucker (1992) 'Managing for the Future', Butterworth-Heinemann. Pp100-103.

than Dash. He writes that leadership is not about having charisma or about having specific leadership qualities or leadership personality.

Leadership is about action – the act of defining and communicating vision and setting goals and priorities. Leadership must be seen as responsibility rather than a rank and privilege. It is also about creating 'human energies and human vision'.

Above all he stresses the importance of trust. *"To trust a leader, it is not necessary to like him. Nor is it necessary to agree with him. Trust is the conviction that the leader means what he says, it is a belief in something very old-fashioned, called 'integrity'. A leader's actions and a leader's professed beliefs must be congruent, or at least compatible. Effective leadership – and again this is very old wisdom – is not based on being clever; it is based primarily on being consistent."*[64]

Drucker also has something to say about knowledge workers and their motivation. In his book[65] he writes *"Finally there are the knowledge workers, and especially, the advanced knowledge workers. They have to be 'knowledge professionals'. This means that no one can motivate them. They have to motivate themselves. No one can direct them. They have to direct themselves. After all, no one can supervise them. They are the guardians of their own standards, performance, and objectives. They can be productive only if they are responsible for their own job."*

Druker on managing people – final words

He says there are three traditional approaches to managing people. They are the welfare approach which he says is about *helping* rather than *managing* people. There is the personnel management approach

---

64 Ibid. Pp103.

65 Peter Drucker (1974) 'Management'. Heinemann. Pp242.

which he says " bears the same relationship to managing people as vacuuming the living room and washing the dishes bear to a happy marriage and bringing up of children". The personnel approach addresses hygiene factors (Herzberg's theory – chapter six). Then there is the cost approach which is focused on controlling cost.

However, to manage people effectively requires the leadership of people, a leader who truly believes that *our greatest asset is our people."*

Lessons learnt from Peter Drucker

- Treat people as human beings not as a general resource.

- Consider the two-sided 'psychological contract' when recruiting staff.

- Think things through very carefully before selecting your staff.

- Do not simply focus on a chosen few to develop talent within your organisation. The survival of your business depends on all your employees.

- Set stretch objectives for your staff.

- Motivate your staff not with 'sticks and carrots' but with respect and consideration.

- Make your staff responsible for the work they do.

- As leaders communicate your vision and lead by example. Leadership is about action.

- Institutionalise trust in order to create a collaborative and enabling culture.

- Remember your only greatest asset is people.

SEVENTEEN
Managing people issues in practice

There are many organisations and consultancy and training companies which provide training programmes and advice to all kinds and all sizes of business. Many organisations need such help. In the UK, for example, the Work Foundation (formerly known as the Industrial Society) *'exists to inspire and deliver improvements to performance through improving the quality of working life'.*

The other key organisation, Investors in People, provide national ownership of the Investors in People Standard. The Standard is *'the business improvement tool designed to advance an organisation performance through its employees'.* The focus is on business success through people. An insight into the Standard supports the view that people are indeed our greatest asset.

The Investors in People Standard

Principle 1: Commitment

An Investor in People is fully committed to developing its people in order to achieve its aims and objectives.

INDICATOR I

The organisation is committed to supporting the development of its people.

Evidence:

- Top management can describe strategies that they have put in place to support the development of people in order to improve the organisation performance.

- Managers can describe specific actions that they have taken and are currently taking to support the development of people.

- People can confirm that the specific strategies and actions described by top management and managers take place.

- People believe the organisation is genuinely committed to supporting their development.

INDICATOR II

People are encouraged to improve their own and other people's performance.

Evidence:

- People can give examples of how they have been encouraged to improve their own performance.

- People can give examples of how they have been encouraged to improve other people's performance.

INDICATOR III

People believe their contribution to the organisation is recognised.

Evidence:

- People can describe how their contribution to the organisation is recognised.

- People believe that their contribution to the organisation is recognised.

- People receive appropriate and constructive feedback on a timely and regular basis.

The organisation is committed to ensuring equality of opportunity in the development of its people.

Evidence:

- Top management can describe strategies that they have put in place to ensure equality of opportunity in the development of people.

- Managers can describe specific actions that they have taken and are currently taking to ensure equality of opportunity in the development of people.

- People confirm that the specific strategies and actions described by top management and managers take place and recognise the needs of different groups.

- People believe the organisation is genuinely committed to ensuring equality of opportunity in the development of people.

Principle 2: Planning

An Investor in People is clear about its aims and its objectives and what its people need to do to achieve them.

INDICATOR V

The organisation has a plan with clear aims and objectives which are understood by everyone.

Evidence:

- The organisation has a plan with clear aims and objectives.

- People can consistently explain the aims and objectives of the organisation at a level appropriate to their role.

- Representative groups are consulted about the organisation aims and objectives.

The development of people is in line with the organisation aims and objectives.

Evidence:

- The organisation has clear priorities which link the development of people to its aims and objectives at organisation, team and individual level.

- People clearly understand what their development activities should achieve, both for them and the organisation.

INDICATOR VII

People understand how they contribute to achieving the organisation aims and objectives.

Evidence:

- People can explain how they contribute to achieving the organisation aims and objectives.

Principle 3: Action

An Investor in People develops its people effectively in order to improve its performance.

INDICATOR VIII

Managers are effective in supporting the development of peopl The organisation makes sure that managers have the knowledge and skills they need to develop their people.

Evidence:

- Managers at all levels understand what they need to do to support the development of people.

- People understand what their manager should be doing to support their development.

- Managers at all levels can give examples of actions that they have taken and are currently taking to support the development of people.

- People can describe how their managers are effective in supporting their development.

People learn and develop effectively.

Evidence:

- People who are new to the organisation, and those new to a job, can confirm that they have received an effective induction.

- The organisation can show that people learn and develop effectively.

- People understand why they have undertaken development activities and what they are expected to do as a result.

- People can give examples of what they have learnt (knowledge, skills and attitude) from development activities.

- Development is linked to relevant external qualifications or standards (or both), where appropriate.

Principle 4: Evaluation

An Investor in People understands the impact of its investment in people on its performance.

The development of people improves the performance of the organisation, teams and individuals.

Evidence:

- The organisation can show that the development of people has improved the performance of the organisation, teams and individuals.

INDICATOR XI

People understand the impact of the development of people on the performance of the organisation, teams and individuals. Top management understands the overall costs and benefits of the development of people and its impact on performance.

Evidence:

- People can explain the impact of their development on their performance, and the performance of their team and the organisation as a whole.

INDICATOR XII

The organisation gets better at developing its people

Evidence:

- People can give examples of relevant and timely improvements that have been made to development activities.

Case Studies

The kind of cases and issues the Investors in People have dealt with are presented below:

Manningham City Council – Melbourne, Australia

INTRODUCTION

The city of Manningham is set in the eastern suburbs of Melbourne and covers an area of 113 square kilometers. The Council has a budget of $65 million, a chief executive, four directors and 16 service unit managers. It covers nearly 41,000 dwellings.

THE CHALLENGE

Investors in People was chosen as it offered the best route for managing the people-related aspects of quality. Gordon Hill, acting corporate development manager, believes that the Standard dovetails effectively with other standards such as ISO 9001, ISO 14001 and the local Safety Map certification, which the Council gained earlier. He describes gaining Investor in People recognition as 'the last frontier' in the Council's drive to improve performance across all areas of operation. He sees the Standard as:

- increasing management effectiveness through its people;

- supporting the achievement of key performance indicators;

- creating staff ownership of the corporate plan; and

- ensuring that individual service units meet wider performance standards.

The Investor in People Standard was adopted as a vital piece in the quality jigsaw the Council was assembling, as it was felt other standards neglected the people development element of the task.

THE STRATEGY

The Council established an internal Investor in People team which was responsible for implementing the project and maintaining a strategic overview of the whole process. It also advised individual service units on their action plans and developed a communications plan. The process was piloted with three units before being rolled out to the remaining fourteen.

THE RESULTS

Investors in People has helped the Council to achieve its perennial goal of getting the same output for less cost – without neglecting the human consequences in the process.

The recruitment and retention of 'top level performers' can be an issue in the Australian public service sector. By introducing better employee development processes and giving a top down signal that people really are its most important asset, Manningham City Council has been able to improve motivation, increase customer satisfaction and reduce costs. Low staff turnover levels of only 12% and customer satisfaction ratings of 98% are both attributed in part to Investors in People.

Gordon Hill continues, "The idea of linking staff work processes to the long-term plans for the organisation was long overdue. In our drive to achieve quality across all areas, Investors in People has helped us to create focus in our people development strategy."

Since gaining Investor in People recognition, the Council has been keen to build on its success and maintain the positive momentum. One result is the new *Character First* programme, whereby staff are recognised for who they are and how they go about their job, rather than for what they produce.

Gordon Hill believes that there is a growing awareness of the value of Investors in People in the Australian public sector as a whole. The Council has been contacted by a number of other organisations eager to learn more about its Investor in People journey.

"There seems to be a genuine recognition that a programme of people development will lead to better business performance – a swing towards realising that hiring, retaining and developing high calibre staff will assist in the achievement of business goals. We are happy to tell other organisations that we count our focus on staff development and its integration into our corporate plan as a real strength. Investors in People represented a logical next step in our quality journey. People issues generally arose as major business alignment and efficiency problems that could be addressed through the Standard."

Anglesey Sea Zoo

THE ORGANISATION

Anglesey Sea Zoo is an outstanding visitor attraction, situated on the stunning Isle of Anglesey coastline, close to the village of Brynsien-cyn. Established in 1983 by Alison & David Lea-Wilson, the Sea Zoo evolved from a previous business, Mona Sea Foods, which had operated as a seafood, fish and game wholesaling company, supplying customers throughout North Wales and the North West of England.

Aware of the visitor interest generated by the live oyster and lobster stocks held for wholesaling, the owners purchased additional tanks to exhibit more specimens and made enquiries about grant funding to develop this side of the business. Unable to secure financial support for the project, they decided to continue with development themselves and invested substantial sums in improving the quality of exhibition and support facilities. The business has gone from strength to strength since then.

Anglesey Sea Zoo is open 7 days a week, from March to November, providing visitors with access to a variety of underwater habitats, with displays including a ray pool; lobster lair; fish forest; life under the pier and shipwreck. The Centre offers many related attractions, including 'pearl fishing', a gift shop, water games, children's go-karts, a coffee shop and picnic facilities.

The business currently employs four core members of staff, with numbers rising to 20 during the busy holiday periods. Anglesey Sea Zoo's stated aims and objectives are to develop innovative and exciting products, to promote conservation, to increase income and to provide employees with a good place to work.

Alison & David Lea-Wilson have recently developed a sister business, Halen Mon, which harvests, packs and distributes premium-quality sea salt to over 100 outlets around the world, from its premises at the Sea Zoo.

THE CHALLENGE

In 1994 Alison & David Lea-Wilson's partner in the Sea Zoo decided to leave, offering them the option of buying him out. This was seen as a crucial time for the business and one when decisions about its future direction and potential profitability would have to be made.

Keen to introduce a more structured approach to business development, Alison & David become aware of Investors in People through a management development project in which they were going to ensure that they had the right processes and staff skills to take them there.

THE STRATEGY

- Alison & David produced a business plan, which clearly identified what they wanted to achieve and helped to communicate their vision and objectives to staff working at the Sea Zoo.

- An organisation chart and clear job descriptions, detailing people's responsibilities and areas of accountability, were developed, which helped people to understand the importance of their contribution to the business.

- A structured process for recruitment and selection was introduced, which enable the owners to target their recruitment and to clarify why they were recruiting people and exactly what they needed them to be able to do.

- A formal induction process was developed, incorporating a period of work experience in each department and a comprehensive staff handbook.

- National Vocational Qualifications (NVQs) were introduced for all staff, ensuring that people were trained to industry standards and motivating individuals by offering them formal recognition for their knowledge and skills.

- Evaluation processes were introduced, which looked at how effective training and development activity had been and, also, what customers thought of the service they were receiving from staff.

Anglesey Sea Zoo was first recognised as an Investor in People in February 1996. The organisation successfully retained recognition when it was reviewed in February 1999 and will shortly be going through its 2nd Post Recognition Review.

THE BENEFITS

Anglesey Sea Zoo has won a number of awards for the quality of its service and the development of its business and staff, these include:

- Gold Medal for Services to Tourism.

- Investors in People UK 'Top Training Tip' award, resulting in free attendance at a 3-day Cranfield Business School course.

- A National Tourism Training award, resulting in a £5,000 cash prize.

GOOD PRACTICE EXAMPLES

- To help develop the business further, the Sea Zoo held a 'Business Analysis Meeting', involving all staff, at which all aspect of operations was discussed. Staff reflected upon how things looked and felt at every stage, from the customer's point of view, and then brainstormed how things could be improved, which generated over 100 new ideas.

- The business also carried out a 'Job Swap' exercise, which involved Aquarium staff (employed to feed fish) and Coffee Shop staff (employed to feed people), swapping roles for a shift. The results were startling. Many new ideas and common approaches that were suggested were subsequently implemented.

Diehl Controls UK Ltd

THE ORGANISATION

Diehl Controls Ltd in North Wales was established in April 2000, as an autonomous arm of the German company, Ako/Diehl Controls, Wangen. The business operates as a full service supplier to GDA Ltd and is based within the company's Kimmel Park factory at Bodelwyddan.

Diehl Controls is responsible for the logistics, assembly, programming, testing and delivery of control assemblies to GDA's washing machine production lines. It is also responsible for the warranty on the product.

The business operates under the direction of a Plant Manager, assisted by two Supervisors, two Quality Engineers, one Logistics Planner, two Team Leaders, two Materials Handlers and a team of 12 Operators; working a two shift pattern.

THE CHALLENGE

From the outset, the management of Diehl Controls recognised that the Company's stated philosophy of continual improvement would be potentially difficult to implement, due to its excellent new facilities and the high quality of component parts, supplied by its German parent company. Development of people was soon identified as one area where the company could focus its improvement efforts, in an attempt to establish added value for its key client, so ensuring total customer satisfaction.

Although managers within the business had an abundance of engineering, quality and technical skills and experience, few had received formal training in people management skills, or the development of appropriate related systems and processes.

Diehl Controls identified that all new team recruits would need comprehensive training, to enable them to work in the 'high-tech', multi-skilled environment, demanded by their new employers. Management wanted to create a culture where people felt well informed, able to actively contribute and confident in their skills and abilities. They saw Investors in People as a key way of achieving these things.

Using Investors in People helped the organisation to plan its training activities and the company continues to use the standard to evaluate the impact of its investment in the team's performance.

THE STRATEGY

- The Investors in People process was explained to all staff, at a specially convened meeting, and people were asked for their support in working towards achievement of the Standard.

- Investors in People Working Group was established, to help with development of systems and processes and to ensure that employees were kept informed of developments, through their Employee Representative.

- The Company produced a training plan, which identified staff skills and distribution required to meet projected targets for the business.

- Training matrices were created, which showed, at a glance, which employees had been trained in which skills, who was considered competent and who was able to train others.

- An employee Committee was set up, to encourage effective communication between management and staff.

- Diehl Control identified what support was available locally, to help with the financing and delivery of training and development for staff (e.g.: Individual Learning Accounts).

- Individual reviews were introduced for all employees, providing them with the opportunity to discuss their performance and to agree upon objective and development needs.

- Team meetings were launched, to keep people informed of the Company's performance and as a forum to discuss issues and to make improvement suggestions.

- Staff surveys were carried out, to gauge how people felt about new processes being introduced and how effective they were at meeting people's development needs.

- Brainstorming sessions were carried out with employees, to encourage involvement and ownership of business improvement at all levels and to generate new ideas to deal with operational issues.

INVESTORS IN PEOPLE HISTORY

Diehl Controls UK Ltd was recognised as an Investor in People, following its first assessment in September 2001.

THE BENEFITS

- The Company have met all production targets and introduced many additional value added services to their Customer in its first 18 months of operation.

- Diehl Controls is consistently achieving the customer satisfaction, quality and revenue targets, agreed with its parent company and major client.

- Achieving Investors in People has enabled the Company to meet its parent company's internal people development standards.

(Source: Investors in People, UK, 7-10 Chandos Street, London, WIG 9DQ.)

The previous cases emphasise the importance of managing people effectively in achieving your organisational objectives. These cases range from small to large organisations and spread across national and international boundaries.

EIGHTEEN
Great companies to work for: the people management perspective

In January, 2004, Fortune published its findings on '10 Great Companies to Work For'. It wrote *"Through ten companies in ten countries, one theme ran like a strong thread in our effort to find a great European workplace: Employees like working for a company with a distinctive culture and a clear social mission."*

So what are the key attributes of the 'winning' companies/organisations?

- People are happy to be there.

- Humour and friendliness.

- Nice treatment.

- Diversity.

- Empowerment to meet customers' needs.

- Contributing to the social cause.

- Flexible work schedules.

- Taking care of its workers.

- Intellectual challenge.

- Talent development strategy.

- Encouraging career planning.

- Employees have a sense of excitement.

- Egalitarian culture.

- Balance between the private and personal life.

- Learning culture.

- People are appreciated.

In 2003, The Sunday Times published the list of 100 best companies to work for. These companies were best to work for because according to their employees:

- They put people before profit.

- People are treated fairly.

- There is a flexible working culture.

- Caring attitude to employees.

- Leaders as excellent role models.

- Supporting good causes.

- Respect for staff.

Conclusions: (drawn from both *Fortune* and *The Sunday Times* surveys) **Highly motivated people contribute to highly satisfied customers and to successful business performance.**

Managing people issues at Prêt A Manger

Employer branding at Prêt A Manger

Esther O'Halloran, MAPD, Recruitment & Retention Manager, Prêt A Manger, UK.

At MCE's 34th Global human resource management conference in April 2002 in Lisbon, Esther O'Halloran provided an insight into *"an innovative consumer brand where creative solutions to attracting and retaining great people can be demonstrated"*.

Prêt A Manger is a privately owned company founded in 1986. It aims to deliver high quality food with a fast, friendly service. It owns and manages all its outlets, *"providing maximum control of the brand and ensuring consistently high standards"*. It has 118 shops in the UK, as well as shops in New York and Hong Kong.

In 1999, its HR and training teams were created.

Prêt A Manger has three core values: Passionate about Food, Passionate about People, Passionate about Prêt. Its vision is *"to build an international business whose customers and employees are appreciated and respected. We can only do this by looking after our food, our people, our customers and Prêt"*. It aspires to a culture of honesty, individualism, openness and support – instilled in its HR systems, and by 'talking, doing, listening, revising, and measuring'. To quote from its 'Career Card', Prêt A Manger is *"determined never to forget that our hardworking people make all the difference. They are our heart and soul. When they care, our business is sound. If they cease to care, our business goes down the drain."* Furthermore, *"we take our reward schemes and career opportunities very seriously. We train and develop. We invest in our people"*. And there is fun: *"We wear jeans, we party, we have great teams"*. Prêt A Manger has an incentives reward and recognition scheme, which includes 'outstanding cards'; individual, team and company bonuses; a £1,000 Holiday Voucher special award; and weekly, summer and Christmas parties. It listens and talks to its staff with daily team briefs, and has an 'open door' policy. Its involves its people in the decision-making process – when recruiting, for example, the shop team approves or disapproves based on aptitude and personality, and is then responsible for training and communication. Prêt A Manger has a young and enthusiastic workforce, increased retention, and an improved skills base through continued experience. Team member applications are rising exponentially. Fortune named it as one of the ten best companies to work for in Europe. For Prêt A Manger, quality is paramount. *"We are passionate about food, our staff, and our customers. If there is a secret to our success so far, it's probably our determination to put quality ahead of profit. Quality, not just of our food, but in every aspect of what we do"*.

(Source: Management Centre Europe, Rue de l'Aqueduc 118, B-1050, Brussels. E-News letter.)

NINETEEN
A to Z of managing people

A   Align your staff objectives with corporate objectives.

B   Build trust and collaborative culture.

C   Communicate, coach and create a thriving work environment.

D   Develop talent at all levels not just for the chosen few.

E   Energise your staff to achieve corporate goals and to take responsibility.

F   Facilitate knowledge sharing within your organisation.

G   Generate enthusiasm and commitment through your leadership.

H   Hierarchical structures should be abolished.

I   Inform, invest, innovate and above all inspire.

J   Justify your actions and decisions.

K   Know your staff and your self.

L   Lead, learn and leverage your staff competencies.

M   Measure, monitor and motivate.

N   Never manage personnel; manage people

O   Open communication contributes to developing trust.

P   Psychological contract should be respected.

Q   Quest for learning should be supported.

R   Recruit and retain your staff.

S   Skills should be continuously updated.

T	Trust is the main driver of managing people effectively.
U	Understand the importance of managing people effectively.
V	Values and vision influence your staff behaviour.
W	Win your staff by your action.
X	X theory assumptions should be eradicated.
Y	Your conviction and commitment will determine your success.
Z	Zeal and zest of your staff should be supported by providing opportunities to perform well.

Prayer

"God grant me courage
to change
the things I can,

The patience to accept the
things I cannot change,
and the wisdom
to know the difference."

Anon

Further reading suggestions

- Argyris, Chris (1985). 'Strategy, Change and Defensive Routines' Pitman.

- Bedeian, Arthur, G. (1980). 'organisations Theory and Analysis'. Holt-Saunders International.

- Bennis, Warren (1989). 'Becoming a Leader'. Hutchinson Business Books.

- Bennis & Goldsmith (1997). 'Learning to Lead'. Nicholas Brealey Publishing.

- Brown, Crainer, Dearlove, Rodrigues (2002). 'Business Minds'. Financial Times/Prentice Hall.

- Carvell, Fred J. (1970). 'Human Relations in Business'. The Macmillan Company.

- Covey, Stephen R (1989) 'The Seven Habits of Highly Effective People'. Simon & Schuster.

- Daft, Richard L. (1998). 'organisation Theory and Design'. South Western College Publishing.

- Drucker, Peter (1966). 'The Effective Executive'. Heinemann Professional Publishing.

- Drucker, Peter (1955). 'The Practice of Management'. Heinemann Professional Publishing.

- Drucker, Peter (1964). 'Managing For Results'. Heinemann Professional Publishing.

- Drucker, Peter (1974). 'Management: Tasks, Responsibilities, Practices'. Heinemann Professional Publishing.

- Harris, Thomas A. (1973). 'I'M OK-YOU@RE OK'. Pan Books.

- Hofstede, Geert (1991) 'Cultures and organisations'. Harper-Collins Publishers.

- Handy, Charles (1989). 'The Age of Unreason'. Business Books.

- Handy, Charles (1995). 'Beyond Certainty'. Hutchinson.

- Handy, Charles (1994). 'The Empty Raincoat'. Hutchinson.

- Handy, Charles (1990). 'Inside organisations'. BBC Books.

- Handy, Charles (1976). 'Understanding organisations'. Penguin Books.

- Huczynski and Buchanan (2001). 'organisational Behaviour'.

- Financial Times Prentice Hall.

- Kanter, Rosabeth Moss (1989). 'When Giants Learn to Dance'. Simon & Schuster.

- Kanter, Rosabeth Moss (1983). 'The Change Masters'. Unwin Paperbacks.

- Kotter, John (1988). 'The Leadership Factor'. The Free Press.

- Kermally, Sultan (1996). 'Total Management Thinking'. Butterworth-Heinemann.

- Kermally, Sultan (1997). 'Managing Performance'. Butterworth-Heinemann.

- Kermally, Sultan (2002). 'Effective Knowledge Management'. John Wiley.

- Kotter, John (1985). 'Power and Influence'. The Free Press.

- Mahesh, V. S. (1993). 'Thresholds of Motivation'. Tata McGraw-Hill Publishing

- Micklewait & Wooldridge (1996). 'The Witch Doctors'. Heinemann.

- Pascale, Richard (1990). 'Managing on the Edge'. Penguin Books.

- Senge, Peter, M (1990). 'The Fifth Discipline'. Century Books.

- Thomas, Mark (1997). 'Mastering People Management'. Thorogood.

- Thomas, Neil (Ed). (1998). 'The John Adair Handbook of Management and Leadership'. Thorogood.

- Vroom, Victor H. (1990). 'Manage People, Not Personnel'. Harvard Business Review Book.

Other titles from Thorogood

DEVELOPING AND MANAGING TALENT
How to match talent to the role and convert it to a strength

Sultan Kermally
£12.99 paperback, £24.99 hardback
Published May 2004

Effective talent management is crucial to business development and profitability. Talent management is no soft option; on the contrary, it is critical to long-term survival.

This book offers strategies and practical guidance for finding, developing and above all keeping talented individuals. After explaining what developing talent actually means to the organization, he explores the e-dimension and the global dimension. He summarizes what the 'gurus' have to say on the development of leadership talent. Included are valuable case studies drawn from Hilton, Volkswagen, Unilever, Microsoft and others.

GURUS ON MARKETING

Sultan Kermally
£14.99 paperback, £24.99 hardback
Published November 2003

Kermally has worked directly with many of the figures in this book, including Peter Drucker, Philip Kotler and Michael Porter. It has enabled him to summarise, contrast and comment on the key concepts with knowledge, depth and insight, and to offer you fresh ideas to improve your own business. He describes the key ideas of each 'guru', places them in context and explains their significance. He shows you how they were applied in practice, looks at their pros and cons and includes the views of other expert writers.

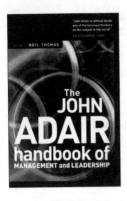

THE JOHN ADAIR HANDBOOK OF MANAGEMENT AND LEADERSHIP

John Adair • Edited by Neil Thomas
£12.99 paperback, £24.99 hardback
Published April 2004

"A book for constant reference ... A great achievement ...ought to be found on every manager's bookshelf."
JOURNAL OF THE INSTITUTE OF PUBLIC SECTOR MANAGEMENT

"... without doubt one of the foremost thinkers on the subject in the world." SIR JOHN HARVEY-JONES

A master-class in managing yourself and others, it combines in one volume all of Adair's thought and writing on leadership, teambuilding, creativity and innovation, problem solving, motivation and communication.

SUCCESSFUL BUSINESS PLANNING

Norton Paley
£14.99 paperback, £29.99 hardback
Published June 2004

"Growth firms with a written business plan have increased their revenues 69 per cent faster over the past five years than those without a written plan."
FROM A SURVEY BY PRICEWATERHOUSECOOPERS

We know the value of planning – in theory. But either we fail to spend the time required to go through the thinking process properly, or we fail to use the plan effectively. Paley uses examples from real companies to turn theory into practice.

THE SHORTER MBA
A practical approach to the key business skills

Barrie Pearson and Neil Thomas
£35.00 Hardback
Published July 2004

A succinct distillation of the skills that you need to be successful in business. Most people can't afford to give up two years to study for an MBA. This pithy, practical book presents all the essential theory, practice and techniques taught to MBA students – ideal for the busy practising executive. It is divided into three parts:

1. Personal development

2. Management skills

3. Business development

GURUS ON BUSINESS STRATEGY

Tony Grundy
£14.99 paperback, £24.99 hardback
Published May 2003

This book is a one-stop guide to the world's most important writers on business strategy. It expertly summarises all the key strategic concepts and describes the work and contribution of each of the leading thinkers in the field.

It goes further: it analyses the pro's and con's of many of the key theories in practice and offers two enlightening case-studies. The third section of the book provides a series of detailed checklists to aid you in the development of your own strategies for different aspects of the business.

More than just a summary of the key concepts, this book offers valuable insights into their application in practice.

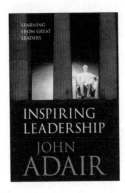

INSPIRING LEADERSHIP

Learning from great leaders

John Adair
£15.99 paperback, £24.99 hardback
Published January 2003

'I discovered once again how rare it is to come upon a book about leaders with depth, conceptual bite and historical context. It was a relief and joy'.

WARREN BENNIS, US MAJOR LEADERSHIP GURU

'I believe it is a 'must read' book... He is without doubt one of the foremost thinkers on the subject in the world.'

SIR JOHN HARVEY-JONES, PREVIOUSLY CEO OF ICI

Great leaders from Lao Tzu, Machiavelli and Washington to Thatcher, Mandela and Reagan are not only great leaders in history, they also have much to teach us today about the nature and practice of leadership. Adair uncovers their different facets of leadership in this heavily illustrated book.

Thorogood also has an extensive range of reports and special briefings which are written specifically for professionals wanting expert information.

For a full listing of all Thorogood publications, or to order any title, please call Thorogood Customer Services on 020 7749 4748 or fax on 020 7729 6110. Alternatively view our website at **www.thorogoodpublishing.co.uk**.

falconbury

BUSINESS SEMINARS

Focused on developing your potential

Falconbury, the sister company to Thorogood publishing, brings together the leading experts from all areas of management and strategic development to provide you with a comprehensive portfolio of action-centred training and learning.

We understand everything managers and leaders need to be, know and do to succeed in today's commercial environment. Each product addresses a different technical or personal development need that will encourage growth and increase your potential for success.

- Practical public training programmes
- Tailored in-company training
- Coaching
- Mentoring
- Topical business seminars
- Trainer bureau/bank
- Adair Leadership Foundation

The most valuable resource in any organisation is its people; it is essential that you invest in the development of your management and leadership skills to ensure your team fulfil their potential. Investment into both personal and professional development has been proven to provide an outstanding ROI through increased productivity in both you and your team. Ultimately leading to a dramatic impact on the bottom line.

With this in mind Falconbury have developed a comprehensive portfolio of training programmes to enable managers of all levels to develop their skills in leadership, communications, finance, people management, change management and all areas vital to achieving success in today's commercial environment.

What Falconbury can offer you?

- Practical applied methodology with a proven results
- Extensive bank of experienced trainers
- Limited attendees to ensure one-to-one guidance
- Up to the minute thinking on management and leadership techniques
- Interactive training
- Balanced mix of theoretical and practical learning
- Learner-centred training
- Excellent cost/quality ratio

Falconbury In-Company Training

Falconbury are aware that a public programme may not be the solution to leadership and management issues arising in your firm. Involving only attendees from your organisation and tailoring the programme to focus on the current challenges you face individually and as a business may be more appropriate. With this in mind we have brought together our most motivated and forward thinking trainers to deliver tailored in-company programmes developed specifically around the needs within your organisation.

All our trainers have a practical commercial background and highly refined people skills. During the course of the programme they act as facilitator, trainer and mentor, adapting their style to ensure that each individual benefits equally from their knowledge to develop new skills.

Falconbury works with each organisation to develop a programme of training that fits your needs.

Mentoring and coaching

Developing and achieving your personal objectives in the workplace is becoming increasingly difficult in today's constantly changing environment. Additionally, as a manager or leader, you are responsible for guiding colleagues towards the realisation of their goals. Sometimes it is easy to lose focus on your short and long-term aims.

Falconbury's one-to-one coaching draws out individual potential by raising self-awareness and understanding, facilitating the learning and performance development that creates excellent managers and leaders. It builds renewed self-confidence and a strong sense of 'can-do' competence, contributing significant benefit to the organisation. Enabling you to focus your energy on developing your potential and that of your colleagues.

Mentoring involves formulating winning strategies, setting goals, monitoring achievements and motivating the whole team whilst achieving a much improved work life balance.

Falconbury – Business Legal Seminars

Falconbury Business Legal Seminars specialises in the provision of high quality training for legal professionals from both in-house and private practice internationally.

The focus of these events is to provide comprehensive and practical training on current international legal thinking and practice in a clear and informative format.

Event subjects include, drafting commercial agreements, employment law, competition law, intellectual property, managing an in-house legal department and international acquisitions.

For more information on all our services please contact Falconbury on +44 (0) 20 7729 6677 or visit the website at: www.falconbury.co.uk.